PEINÁO

A Greek Feast for All

Parea (n.)
παρέα

A Greek word meaning a close group
of friends who gather together purely
to enjoy each other's company and share
life experiences, values and ideas.

This book is dedicated to our beautiful mum, Sophie. Without you we wouldn't be where we are today – thank you for always reminding us that 'we got this'.

And to Yiayia Koula, you taught us how to fold a sentóni (bed sheet), iron (basically everything), make pastitsio and, most importantly, how to love and treat everyone like they are family.

HELENA & VIKKI
MOURSELLAS

PEINÁO
A Greek Feast for All

RECIPES TO FEED HUNGRY GUESTS

Smith
Street
Books

CONTENTS

INTRODUCTION

Yasou. Helena and Vikki here. Firstly, a very BIG efharisto (thank you) for giving *Peináo* a cosy place to live in your home – it means the world to us.

For us, food memories are held very close to our hearts. It's incredible how many times a recipe of Yiayia's or Mum's has saved us from wanting to get into bed and cry because we are homesick. With one mouthful, we are back at Yiayia's stovetop eating spaghetti from the pot and listening to Aliki Vougiouklaki on the TV, and we instantly feel safe and content.

Growing up in an Australian-Greek family home in Adelaide, South Australia, meant our home was always filled with family, friends, laughter, tears and, of course, lots of delicious food. We grew up attending family social events nearly every weekend, from cousins' birthday parties to Greek weddings and Saturday night barbecues. Tables would be filled with trays of pastitsio, bowls of garlicky tzatziki, platters of diamond-cut pieces of revani and glasses of homemade red wine from Mum's uncle Harry. Sometimes there would be three of the same cake sitting on the table from three different aunties. Mum and Dad loved entertaining – ours was the house that everyone would pop over to for a wine and a plate of olives, and Dad's freshly caught fish. The kids would run wild around the house playing hide and seek, while the adults enjoyed a drink and listened to Greek music. This is when the love for entertaining started for us.

We were very fortunate to have Yiayia and Papou raise us alongside Mum and Dad. While Mum and Dad were working, Yiayia and Papou would arrive at our house every morning around 6 am. Yiayia knew exactly what she would be cooking for the day, while Papou mowed the lawns. Papou would drop off fish and chips to us at school for lunch, and our friends were always amazed that he would do that. He even once fell asleep in the car and someone called the police ... hehe ... he loved an afternoon nap.

When we are homesick we always make Yiayia's cheesy garlic and butter makaronia and memories of her in her apron, stirring the cheese into the makaronia, come flooding back.

Yiayia and Papou had a couple of mandarin trees and a fig tree with the jammiest and sweetest figs we have ever tasted. Papou Vasilis was a painter, and we would drag his painting ladder through the grass to pick the figs and mandarins from the trees. Even today, if we smell freshly picked mandarins, we cry instantly – we've even cried in the fruit aisle at the supermarket. A supermarket fig will never come close to the ones we grew up eating.

When we were 12 years old, our father died suddenly, he was only 41. We were given meals from our neighbours, friends and family who came to visit us during this hard time. A plate of food meant so much to Mum, it was a gift, and it brought a sense of safety and comfort. Yiayia and Papou stepped in and became our rock. Mum worked full-time while Yiayia and Papou looked after us, and without them we wouldn't have had the support we needed – Mum was so grateful. Yiayia taught us how to cook; she showed us how to make food with our hearts and our hands. We loved everything she made for us, and Mum would get upset when we said Yiayia's food was better than hers. Yiayia also taught us how to mop, vacuum, fold tea towels, iron clothes (she used to iron our underwear and pyjamas) and clean windows. We absolutely loved it. (Sounds mad, right? What kids like doing chores? We did and still do!) Papou Vasíllis taught us to paint; he also tried to teach us to be patient (that never worked).

After Dad passed away, Mum showed us how to be strong women and that life could go on. She made sure we were always surrounded by positive people and delicious food. Everyone loved Mum's cooking; it brought her joy and it made us happy to see her full of life again. As a family, cooking saved us – we suffered with anxiety as children and even as adults – losing our Dad at a young age was tough and, of course, tougher for Mum. But when we came together to make food, our worries disappeared and all we had to do, in that moment, was cook with happiness and love.

Living at home with Mum was like living at a hotel, with free food, bedding and WIFI (a very good and cheap deal). She only started charging us rent at the ripe age of 22. When we did move out of home we moved states, which was very hard for her. We drove the 654 km to Melbourne in our little Mitsubishi red Colt, packed with our favourite cookbooks, some clothes and our friend Katie. We arrived with only $200 in our bank accounts, so we shared a room to save money. Initially, we were quite lost with what career paths to take, but we always knew Dad wanted us to follow our hearts. Vikki studied graphic design, worked at a cafe during the day as a waitress (she couldn't even hold three plates) and as a bartender at night. She even got a job in retail selling shoes. Helena worked at a Jewish deli and studied radio. We shared a house with friends from Adelaide and a couple of expats from London. Hosting dinner parties on a low budget was always a fun challenge, and the thought of feeding hungry people with very little money got us excited.

For both of us, we always felt we weren't 'good enough' because we didn't go to university like many of our peers, but losing Dad distracted us ... it was a tough time. Our lives changed completely when we received a phone call from Channel 7 asking if we would like to take part in the TV show *My Kitchen Rules*. Helena had entered us for three years in a row, but we never made the cut. We will never forget the moment they called us and said, 'This might be your year!' We laughed at each other and said, 'Yeah, right!' So we both pulled a sick day and went for the audition in the city. We put on our best clothes and prayed to Dad to make this dream come true. A couple of days later they called us to say we had made it through the first rounds; the next stage was to cook at home with a camera crew filming us. We had to pay our housemates $15 each to leave the house for the day. The drama started only minutes into cooking, the smoke alarm went off and Vikki was jumping around trying to stop it, while Helena was thinking, that's it, it's over! Funnily enough, the drama is what got us through!

A couple of weeks later, we were driving home from Queen Victoria Market when we received a call from the *My Kitchen Rules* team. We both started to scream with excitement and nervousness, we weren't ready to be rejected for a fourth time. Helena answered the phone and the producer said, 'Congrats, you girls have been selected; oh, and you are also the Victoria team.' First of all we were shocked that we were finally going to be on the show, but it was an even bigger shock to be told we were representing a state we had only lived in for four months. We don't believe in luck, but we do believe in ourselves. We weren't lucky that we got onto *My Kitchen Rules*, we had earned it. It was passion and hard work that gave us the opportunity, and we knew that if we could eventually make money doing something we absolutely love, then we would be living our best lives.

We kept paying rent on our Melbourne apartment and flew to Sydney to film the show. We spent six months filming and travelling the country, visiting the other contestants' homes. Obviously, dinner parties on TV are very different from real life, but we love that we got to show Australia how we throw a big fat Greek dinner party.

Soon after *My Kitchen Rules* we moved to Sydney. The show had opened a whole other world to us and gave us opportunities for which we are forever grateful. Helena took to cheffing and started working for renowned chef Colin Fassnidge at 4Fourteen. She was super passionate and stuck it out for four years. Fifteen-hour days, a kitchen full of men – it was a hard industry, but she pushed through and managed to find a deep love for it. Vikki gave the chef life a go but knew it wasn't for her; instead, she dreamed of working in publishing, which Helena never understood until one day Vikki started freelancing and recipe writing for different publishing houses. That's when Helena jumped on board and got a job at *delicious.* magazine as assistant food editor. It's been her dream job ever since.

Throughout our time on *My Kitchen Rules* we started to write recipes for our first cookbook *Taking You Home: Simple Greek Food*, which was published in 2015. When we moved to Sydney the idea for *Peináo* came alive – we had always dreamed of writing a book about feeding hungry guests. Helena had moved into a four-bedroom house in Surry Hills – it was the place to be if you wanted to chat about life, dance in the backyard or have a cry in your bathrobe.

We would throw the best house parties and the food we served was whatever we brought home from our jobs working as a photo chef and food editor. We've always believed that food brings people together. We love feeding everyone and anyone. Going to bed with smiles on our faces knowing we have fed someone something yummy and made them feel warm and loved – that is truly our purpose.

'Peináo' means 'I'm hungry' in Greek. How many times in your life have you said this out loud? It is an absolute joy for us to hear people say it, and we feel like heroes when we are there to save someone from becoming 'hangry'. Our table is always filled with friends and family and whoever else decides to join at the last minute. Hosting a lunch or dinner should not be stressful, it should involve dancing in your fluffy slippers while stirring a pot of bolognese and singing out loud. This is what we call fun, not a chore.

Who said you can't throw a dinner party on a Tuesday night? It doesn't matter if you're hosting a simple midweek meal for four or an extravagant weekend feast for ten, *Peináo* will guide you through your menu. We want to be there to cook with you, like it's the best moment of your day. *Peináo* can live in all the places of your home: the dining table, kitchen bench, coffee table, bar trolley, guest house, bedside table, bathtub or simply on your bookshelf.

We hope *Peináo* brings love and joy to your table, to inspire you to cook with your heart and remember how special it is to share food with your favourite people. So, get to the kitchen and start cooking, have fun, play your favourite music, dance around the kitchen table and remember that life is short, so may we eat good food with great people, and never count the calories. Kalí órexi!

Helena and Vikki xx

HOW TO PLAN BEFORE GUESTS ARRIVE

Our style for throwing a dinner party changes every week depending on what day it is, the mood we are in, how busy we have been at work, the season, who we're inviting over … We host most of our dinner parties at Helena's house, as our most frequent guests already live there and we know people will be coming in and out to stay for a mezze or arrive just in time for dessert.

Here are some of the simple ways we like to prepare before our guests arrive. Remember, entertaining should be fun, not stressful!

MENU

Planning a menu and writing a prep list is really important and a great way to stay on top of everything. We usually spend the day before writing our menu and going through the fridge to see what ingredients can be used up. This not only eliminates food waste but keeps costs down. Cleaning out your fridge a couple of days before your gathering also gives you more space to store any pre-prepared dishes. Leaving a whole shelf free in the fridge is handy, but we know this is sometimes impossible – Helena has lived in a share house for seven years, so we are professionals at fridge Tetris.

Remember that *Peináo* is about sharing and throwing a bunch of dishes in the middle of the table for everyone to help themselves. If you're hosting a breakfast, for example, make sure the recipes you choose can be prepped the day before or can be made easily in the morning before everyone arrives. We have included notes in most of our recipes, telling you which elements can be prepared ahead of time.

Playing some zen tunes while prepping ingredients is one of our favourite things to do – if possible, try and kick everyone out of the house for a while, as having some peace and quiet while you cook is key. Try not to drink the booze you are serving, save it and stay on the sodas … Kidding! Have some drinks before everyone arrives.

STYLING

There are a lot of elements that make up a table setting, from the linen to the plates, the glasses and cutlery. Depending on what type of meal you are hosting, how you style your dining table can really help set the vibe. If you are having a chilled dinner party, don't bring out the crystal glasses (we actually don't own crystal glasses) or your fanciest cutlery – keep it relaxed so the style matches the food you are serving. Sometimes we love to keep it minimal, while other times we really take it up a notch and surprise our guests with something fun, such as a colour scheme – we love matching flowers with the colour of linen we are using.

Adding some quirky touches can also be great, such as using clean oyster and scallop shells for a salt bowl and butter dish. Fresh or dried bay leaves or rosemary arranged on dinner plates looks elegant and really adds that extra touch, while cutting into a mandarin and placing a candle inside looks beautiful and helps recreate those hot Greek summer night vibes.

Named place settings can make things more personable – writing your guests' names on some brown paper can be cute. Freshly picked olive branches bring a Mediterranean feel – they sit nicely on the plate with a white or cream napkin. Dehydrated oranges and lemons are also super pretty, and are easy to prepare: simply place finely sliced citrus on a wire rack lined with baking paper and dehydrate in a preheated 90°C (180°F) oven for 1 hour each side or until the fruit is dry but still vibrant. Store in an airtight container for up to 1 month. The dehydrated fruit is also perfect for garnishing cocktails or soda water jugs.

LIGHTING

Getting the lighting right is also very important. Too bright lights, such as kitchen fluorescent lighting, can make you feel like you are in a laundromat ... this is not the vibe we want, and a dark room means your guests won't be able to see what they are eating. You want your lighting to be soft and cosy, while bright enough for your guests to see each other and what's on their plates (remember, we eat with our eyes). Candles bring a very hygge feeling to a dinner party, and walking into a home lit with candles can really set the mood for the evening. Make sure not to buy scented candles as they may overpower the smell of the food. Yes, a caramel slice-scented candle smells yum, but having whiffs of your honey biscuits baking away in the oven is a million times better. Using empty bottles of any new favourite wine as candle holders is a great way to recycle and remember the name of the wine for next time.

For some moody lighting, grab your bedside lamp and place it on the floor in an empty space. If the lamp moves, shine the light towards the ceiling to create a softer ambience.

DRINKS

Choosing drinks for a dinner party can be hard. Consider what will go well with your menu and, of course, what your guests love to drink. Generally, you want to start the night off with something light and easy to drink, such as Champagne. The drinks in our Cheers chapter will match any occasion and our absolute favourite is the Greek negroni (see page 200).

MUSIC

Of course delicious food (and wine) is the key to a successful dinner party, but the music beating out of your speakers is also very important. Have you ever been the first to arrive and there's no music playing? Awkward, right? There's nothing better than your friends arriving to hear their favourite tune blasting from the living room. Making playlists of songs with memories attached to them will have your guests instantly dancing. Start the night off with something calming but upbeat – you want to ease your guests into the night, not put them to sleep.

Matching the music to your menu can be fun. For us, a Greek dinner party means only Greek music. Our non-Greek friends usually end up loving our Greek tunes and there's always a Greek dancing lesson happening by the end of the night. Although, if we're honest, we are not the best Greek dancers but we do try. A funny story: when we were 16, we were bridesmaids at our cousin's wedding and we had to attend Greek dancing lessons every Saturday morning, which we hated. When the time came to dance in front of everyone at the wedding, Yiayia had a group of friends walk up to her and ask why her granddaughters couldn't Greek dance. Awkward!

KITCHEN NOTES

The pantry and fridge staples found in Greek kitchens are the same everyday essentials most of us probably already have. Throughout this book we have used everyday ingredients, apart from a couple of Greek spices, such as mahlepi and mastiha (that you might not have heard of), but we don't expect you to drive around looking for them.

We believe in buying good-quality basic ingredients such as oil, vinegar, honey and cheese. Ten years ago, we were living on a super-low budget, which meant the cheapest of everything went straight into the shopping trolley with zero hesitation. We were still able to cook delicious food using these ingredients, but we knew that good-quality produce makes a big difference. It's taken us until our 30s to earn enough to spend more on staples such as eggs and oil. This takes time to achieve, so don't worry if you're shopping on a budget. We have all been there and done that.

Buying in bulk is the smartest way to buy those good-quality ingredients; yes it might seem expensive to buy 4 litres (qts) of olive oil, but it works out a lot cheaper in the long run. Back in the day, Yiayia and Papou's laundry was like a supermarket, filled with dried beans, tins of tomatoes, bottles of passata (pureed tomatoes) and packets of dried pasta and rice. They would wash and dry jars and ice-cream containers. We were always fooled by what was actually inside – we would open up the biscuit tin to find Yiayia's sewing equipment. Living in a share house can be great for buying pantry items in bulk, as everyone can throw in some money and reap the benefits.

OUR KITCHEN STAPLES

CHEESE
Greek cheeses are readily available at most supermarkets. Alternatively, head to your local Greek delicatessen. Below are the cheeses we have used in this book.

Feta: a crumbly, salty and tangy cheese that is probably the most famous cheese associated with Greece. It is made with sheep's milk and sometimes a combination of sheep and goat's milk.

Galotyri: a soft and creamy curd cheese that has the same consistency as thick yoghurt, with a delightful acidic taste and a yummy milky finish. 'Galo' means 'milk' and 'tyri' means 'cheese'. It is made from 100 per cent Greek pasteurised sheep and goat's milk. In Greece, galotyri is mainly made in summer when milk quality is at its peak.

Graviera: a hard yellow cheese with a nutty and fruity flavour. It is very popular in Greece where it's mainly used for grating over pasta or in pitas, or as an option for saganaki.

Haloumi: a traditional cheese from Cyprus made from a mixture of sheep and goat's milk and sometimes cow's milk. It has a tangy and salty flavour and a texture that can be described as 'squeaky', with a high melting point. You will find haloumi on most menus serving mezze around the world.

Kasseri: a traditional mild-tasting pale-yellow cheese made from unpasteurised sheep's milk and sometimes goat's milk. It has a semi-hard to hard consistency, with a smooth texture and buttery taste. Kasseri has designated PDO status, which means it can only be produced in particular Greek provinces, but it is easily found in European delis and most supermarkets. One of our favourite dishes is grated kasseri on buttery spaghetti, one of Yiayia's classics.

Kefalotyri: a hard and salty light-yellow cheese made from sheep and goat's milk, with a sharp flavour and dry texture. It is often used for saganaki as it fries well, or it is lovely grated over pizza. If you can't find it, feel free to substitute pecorino or graviera. We have the best memories of our papou Vasilis eating slices of kefalotyri with a glass of dark ale, while doing crosswords.

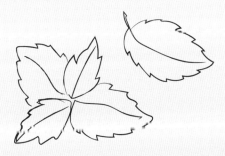

Mizithra: a traditional hard whey cheese, made from a mixture of sheep and goat's whey. Similar to Italian ricotta salata, it's perfect for grating or crumbling on top of pasta or salads.

CITRUS

If there is one ingredient that screams Greece, it's lemon. Lemons take us straight back to Yiayia's kitchen and the aroma of avgolemono soup bubbling away on the stove – see our recipe on page 101. Buying lemons and oranges when they are in season will give you the best-tasting juice. Lemon and orange zest freeze beautifully – simply place the zest in a jar or airtight container and spoon it out whenever a recipe calls for it. As for the juice, squeeze the citrus into ice-cube trays and label with the date. Frozen citrus juice will keep for up to six months and is perfect for making cocktails.

HERBS

Put your hand up if you have stolen herbs from a neighbour's garden? We are guilty of this. Woody herbs, such as rosemary, thyme, oregano and sage, are great for infusing olive oil, or they dry perfectly hanging in your laundry. To dry naturally, simply tie bunches of fresh rosemary or oregano with string and hang upside down in a sunny position for 2–3 weeks. When dried, the leaves should be brittle. Store in a labelled jar or an airtight container away from sunlight for up to a year. They also make great gifts when your friends are having a dinner party. Remember, the stalks of dill, parsley and mint can be finely chopped and added when cooking onion and garlic; they add extra flavour, with no waste. The best way to store fresh herbs is to wrap them in wet paper towel and seal in a zip-lock bag, or place in a jar of water and cover with a large zip-lock bag to create a mini greenhouse.

HONEY

The honey from Greece is considered to be some of the finest in the world, and a favourite among honey connoisseurs. Halkidiki is considered to be the 'motherland' of Greek honey, and the region makes 30 per cent of the country's yearly production. Greek honey is denser and richer compared to other honeys in the world; we use a lot of it in our recipes, especially in our desserts. When purchasing honey, we are mindful of where it has been harvested. We buy ours from a Greek deli, but it can be quite expensive, so we sometimes opt for Australian honey, which is also great – we love Australian bush honey.

JARRED PEPPERS

We use jarred peppers in a lot of our recipes – it's our secret to adding a little extra love. We use pickled golden peppers – both friggitello and pepperoncini peppers, originating in Italy and Greece respectively. The Greek peppers, which are known as the golden Greek pepper variety, are shorter, sweeter and less bitter than the Italian variety, but have a similar heat.

OIL

When Mum would visit us in Melbourne she would want to buy us a present, so we would ask her to buy us olive oil because we had no money. Call us oil snobs but we only use the best-quality Greek extra virgin olive oil (our favourite comes from Northern Greece), and we use it for salad dressings, drizzling over a finished dish and in cakes. For shallow-frying we like to use olive oil or vegetable oil. If you are short on body lotion, head to the pantry and grab yourself some olive oil, it works a treat.

OLIVES

Greece is home to the world's best olives and, of course, olive oil. This is a safe place for us to admit that we only eat olives grown in Greece, particularly from Northern Greece where our family is from. In Yiayia's hometown, Halkidiki, the famous green olive is grown and harvested, and its fruity flavour makes the perfect addition to a mezze. Halkidiki is on the peninsula of Northern Greece, where the land has a unique climate and soil characteristics.

PULSES

Chickpeas (garbanzo beans), yellow split peas, broad (fava) beans and lentils are essential to any Greek pantry. Dried pulses taste better than tinned varieties, but tinned pulses certainly have a place on days when time is limited. Soaking dried pulses overnight removes gas-causing compounds, improves their texture and decreases their cooking time. On Sundays we usually make faki (Greek lentil soup) – we soak dried lentils in water overnight, then saute chopped onion, garlic, carrot, celery and potato in olive oil with some dried oregano, add the lentils and chicken or vegetable stock and simmer. It is seriously the most comforting soup.

SALT

We use good-quality salt flakes for seasoning and fine salt for cooking. We all have different taste buds, so tasting as you cook is really important to achieve the right balance.

TARHANA

One of the oldest foods in the Eastern Mediterranean, tarhana was made as a way to preserve milk for the winter months. There are two types of tarhana: sweet, which uses sheep or goat's milk; and sour, which uses milk and yoghurt. Usually the dairy is combined with wheat and dried in the sun over several days during the hottest month. Once dried, the tarhana is broken into tiny granules and stored in an airtight container, ready to use in winter. It has a similar cooking time to oats and can be eaten for breakfast with goat's milk and fruit, or for dinner, such as our creamy mushroom tarhana on page 102. These days it is quite easy to find tarhana at Greek or European supermarkets. We usually pack a couple of bags in our luggage to bring home from Greece. If you haven't tried it, we encourage you to head out and buy a packet. You will be so surprised at the flavour and texture. Our Aunt Eleni, who lives in Halkidiki, makes her own. We really need to grab the recipe from her.

VINEGAR

A red wine vinegar made exclusively with red wine from Greece is essential in our kitchen. It has a tart and bright flavour profile that will take your salad dressings or pickles to the next level. Greek vinegar is found in most European supermarkets. Our absolute favourite recipe that involves vinegar is so basic that you might think it's boring: boiled cauliflower covered in white vinegar with a little olive oil and salt. It's heaven!

A WORD ON ...

OVEN TEMPERATURES

We have used conventional oven temperatures for the recipes in this book. If using a fan-forced oven, simply reduce the temperature by 20°C (70°F). Every oven works slightly differently depending on the brand, age and whether it is gas or electric. Keep an eye on your dishes as they cook and feel confident to adjust cooking temperatures and times accordingly.

SERVING

The recipes in this book are suitable for any occasion. Most of our breakfast dishes can be served as part of a mezze or even for dinner. We have noted how many people each recipe feeds, and depending on the type of gathering you are hosting we believe it's best to serve a variety of dishes. Mezze, for example, can be served at a cocktail gathering with everyone standing around. We have suggested servings of 4–6, but you know your guests well enough and how much they like to eat. We suggest doubling recipes that serve 4 for groups of 6–8. Having leftovers isn't a bad thing and everyone loves taking food home.

CLEAN-UP TIME

Don't feel bad if your friends offer to help wash up. Having help is great and waking up to a clean kitchen is the best feeling ever. This doesn't work for everyone, however, and sometimes leaving the dishes for the next day is better, especially if you don't want to stay up past midnight cleaning up. And there is something about waking up the next morning and seeing all of last night's fun laid out: empty wine bottles, crumbs scattered all over the tablecloth, candles burnt out. If you have a dishwasher, you are very lucky.

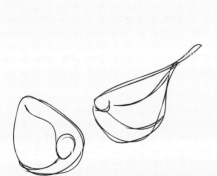

MORNINGS

CHAPTER
01

PROÍ

Kaliméra! This chapter is filled with recipes that will bring sunshine to your morning table. They say the first meal of the day is the most important, and we believe it should be enjoyed with parea (company) and plenty of deliciousness. Yes, we are the people who go to sleep thinking about breakfast and coffee.

We love having friends over for breakfast and, let's face it, eating out can be an expensive event, so why not host your own fabulous morning feast or brunch with a big group of friends or family?

Breakfast in Greece is usually something light and simple that can be eaten on the go. In summer, we're often still up in the early hours, walking home from a nightclub and lining up for a hot, creamy bougatsa after a night of dancing. Well, not every morning! When it's really hot, the first thing we crave is a cold frappe and a plate of sweet, juicy karpoúzi (watermelon). Wintertime involves a cosy sleep-in and watching the snow hit the window while drinking a hot cup of mountain tea and hanging out with Yiayia on the couch – pure bliss.

Most of the recipes in this chapter can be served for a mezze or even for dinner – who doesn't love breakfast at any time of the day?

Tahini pancakes with yoghurt & orange

200 g (1⅓ cups) self-raising flour, sifted

1 teaspoon baking powder

½ teaspoon ground cinnamon

40 g (1½ oz) caster (superfine) sugar

¼ teaspoon salt flakes

50 g (1¾ oz) hulled tahini, plus
    2 teaspoons extra

2 eggs

1 teaspoon honey, plus extra for drizzling

185 ml (¾ cup) full-cream (whole) milk

2 tablespoons unsalted butter, melted

1 orange

375 g (1½ cups) Greek-style yoghurt

~~~~~~~

PREP IS YOUR BEST FRIEND:

The pancake batter can be made in
the morning and stored in the fridge
until guests arrive – simply bring to
room temperature for 30 minutes before
cooking. The orange tahini yoghurt
can be made the day before and stored
in an airtight container in the fridge.

PERFECTLY PAIRED WITH:

Freddo cappuccino (see page 193),
Tsoureki (see page 38) and Avgá me
patátes (see page 29).

Tahini isn't just for making hummus, its nutty flavour and creamy texture
works perfectly in desserts and especially in these pancakes. In Greece,
tahini is usually used for spreading over bread or accompanied with honey
or jam. There are even different flavours of tahini such as chocolate,
orange and honey. When we used to visit Greece, we would pack several
jars to bring back home, but nowadays these flavours are readily available
in Greek supermarkets. If you can get your hands on the orange tahini,
it will change your life.

A breakfast feast without pancakes isn't really breakfast, in our opinion,
and these light and fluffy pancakes will become a trusted recipe you can whip
up whenever you need a quick morning fix. Make sure you give the tahini jar
a good stir first – you want it to be runny and smooth, not lumpy and hard.

In a large bowl, combine the flour, baking powder, cinnamon, sugar and salt
flakes. In a separate bowl, whisk together the tahini, eggs, honey and milk until
combined. Make a well in the centre of the dry ingredients, add the tahini
mixture and whisk until smooth with no lumps remaining.

Heat a large non-stick frying pan over medium heat and brush with some
of the melted butter. Add 60 ml (¼ cup) of the pancake batter to the pan
and cook for 2–3 minutes each side, until lightly golden and cooked through.
Transfer to a plate and cover to keep warm, then repeat with the remaining
batter, adding a little more melted butter as you go.

Zest the orange into a small bowl, add the extra 2 teaspoons of tahini and the
yoghurt and stir to combine.

Peel the orange and cut it into segments, then roughly chop.

Serve the pancakes topped with the orange tahini yoghurt, orange pieces
and a drizzle of extra honey.

Avgá me patátes

EGGS WITH POTATO

vegetable oil, for deep-frying

800 g (1 lb 12 oz) large potatoes,
    such as sebago, peeled and cut
    into 1 cm (½ in) thick chips

salt flakes and freshly cracked
    black pepper

8 eggs

small handful of grated kefalotyri

1 tablespoon oregano leaves, chopped,
    plus extra leaves to serve

2 tablespoons extra virgin olive oil

100 g (3 ½ oz) goat's cheese, crumbled

~~~~~~

PREP IS YOUR BEST FRIEND:

It's best to serve avgá me patátes as soon
as it's ready. The chips can be pre-cut and
left to soak in a bowl of cold water for a
couple of hours before cooking – this not
only prevents the potato from oxidising, it
also gives the chips a better crunch when
fried. Just make sure to pat them dry after
draining to remove any excess water.

If you are short of time, the chips can be
fried the day before and stored at room
temperature in an airtight container,
lined with a piece of paper towel.

PERFECTLY PAIRED WITH:

Lemon thyme psomí (see page 42) and
Greek-style baked beans (see page 44).

This was a classic favourite for Yiayia Koula to whip up after school, a meal
that was quick for her to get on the table for when we arrived home. After a
50-minute bus ride from school and with rumbling tummies, we would hurry
to the front door and run straight to the kitchen to see what Yiayia had cooked.
The kitchen would smell of freshly fried potato chips, and they would be sitting
on a plate lined with paper towel, waiting to be turned into avgá me patátes.
If it was a warm summer's day, the outdoor table would be set up with a plastic
tablecloth and we'd enjoy this simple feast as the fresh summer breeze hit our
cheeks. We can still smell this moment.

The best potatoes to use for the chips are sebago or white brushed
potatoes. Leftover cooked patátes from the day before are also great to use
for this recipe. It might seem a little crazy to make your own potato chips,
but we promise it is so worth it.

Pour enough vegetable oil for deep-frying into a saucepan over low heat and
heat to 180°C (350°F) on a kitchen thermometer. Working in batches, deep-fry
the chips for 10–12 minutes, until lightly golden and crisp. Remove the chips
using a slotted spoon and drain on paper towel to absorb any excess oil. Season
with salt flakes.

Meanwhile, in a bowl, whisk the eggs, cheese and oregano, and season with salt
flakes and cracked black pepper.

Heat the olive oil in a non-stick 26 cm (10¼ in) frying pan over medium heat,
add the chips and pour over the egg mixture. Cook for 8–10 minutes, until the
edge of the egg mixture starts to set. Cover with a large upturned frying pan or
heatproof plate and cook for a further 5 minutes or until the centre of the egg
mixture is cooked through and firm.

Scatter with the goat's cheese and extra oregano leaves, and serve
immediately.

Sesame & fennel seed koulouri

GREEK BREAD RINGS

560 ml (2¼ cups) lukewarm water

7 g sachet (2¼ teaspoons) active
    dried yeast

2 tablespoons honey

450 g (3 cups) plain (all-purpose) flour,
    sifted

75 g (½ cup) wholemeal (whole-wheat)
    self-raising flour

1 teaspoon salt flakes

1 tablespoon caster (superfine) sugar

80 g (½ cup) sesame seeds

30 g (¼ cup) fennel seeds

~~~~~~

PREP IS YOUR BEST FRIEND:
Any baked good is best served hot and
fresh out of the oven, but if you are short
of time the koulouri can be baked the day
before and stored in an airtight container.
Just before serving, reheat the koulouri
in a preheated 150°C (300°F) oven for
20 minutes.

PERFECTLY PAIRED WITH:
Koulouri are also the perfect mezze to
serve during the afternoon. Serve with
Roasted garlic and fennel tzatziki (see
page 62) and Whipped feta, chargrilled
piperiés and almonds (see page 64).
They are also great to mop up all of the
yummy tomatoey bean juices in our
Greek-style baked beans (see page 44).

The famous Greek koulouri of Thessaloniki is sold almost everywhere in
Greece. They are a popular breakfast and you'll find them sold on street
corners – where vendors yell out, 'one euro koulouri!' – and in bakeries.
They're hard to miss.

Koulouri are incredibly crunchy on the outside with a soft and slightly
chewy centre. They are usually eaten on the go, but they also make the perfect
addition to a morning grazing board, served with butter and jams, such as
cherry or fig, or for a savoury vibe, served with olives, tomato, kasseri cheese,
oily fried eggs and, of course, a cold frappe.

Traditionally, koulouri are sprinkled with sesame seeds, but we have
added some fennel seeds because we love them and they add a beautifully
sweet licorice taste. You can omit the fennel seeds to keep them traditional,
if you like.

Line two large baking trays with baking paper.

In a jug, combine 310 ml (1¼ cups) of the lukewarm water with the yeast and
honey. Stir well, then set aside for 10 minutes or until frothy.

Place the flours in the bowl of a stand mixer with the dough hook attached
and stir through the salt flakes. Pour the yeast mixture into the flour and knead
on low speed for 10 minutes or until the dough is smooth and soft.

Rest the dough in a large oiled bowl, covered with a clean tea towel, for 1 hour
or until roughly doubled in size.

Preheat the oven to 200°C (400°F).

Meanwhile, place the sugar and the remaining lukewarm water in a large bowl
and stir for 2 minutes or until the sugar is dissolved. Combine the sesame and
fennel seeds in a separate large bowl.

Divide the dough into ten equal pieces and roll each piece into a 50 cm
(19½ in) long rope. Working with one rope at a time, gently bring the ends
together, overlap them by 2–3 cm (¾–1¼ in) and pinch the dough to seal.

Dip the dough rings into the sugared water, then dip one side into the seed
mixture. Place the dough rings, seed-side up, on the prepared trays and bake
for 20 minutes or until the koulouri are golden and the house smells like
a bakery.

Three cheese tiropita

CHEESE PIE

250 g (9 oz) Greek feta, crumbled

100 g (3½ oz) kasseri cheese, grated

100 g (3½ oz) kefalotyri, grated

2 teaspoons dried mint

2 eggs, lightly beaten

90 g (⅓ cup) Greek-style yoghurt

100 g (3½ oz) unsalted butter, melted,
plus extra for greasing

10 sheets filo pastry

1 tablespoon white sesame seeds

lemon wedges, to serve

~~~~~~~

PREP IS YOUR BEST FRIEND:
The tiropita can be assembled the
day before and stored, covered tightly,
in the fridge overnight.

PERFECTLY PAIRED WITH:
If you'd like to serve the tiropita for
lunch, we think it pairs perfectly with
our OG Greek saláta (see page 133) and
Pork and feta keftedes (see page 81).

'Tiropita' means 'cheese pie' in Greek and consists of layers of buttered filo
pastry and a cheese egg filling. If you have ever wondered about the difference
between a tiropita and a spanakopita, a tiropita has a mixture of Greek
cheeses, whereas a spanakopita has spinach, herbs, such as dill and parsley,
and Greek feta. Both are heavenly.

This recipe calls for store-bought filo pastry, so there is no need to spend
hours making it from scratch; we will leave that for the next book. We have
included this recipe in our morning chapter as it's a popular dish to eat
for breakfast with a frappe, but who said you can't eat it any time of the day?

Preheat the oven to 180°C (350°F).

In a large bowl, combine the cheeses and mint. Add the eggs and yoghurt
and mix until combined.

Grease a 1.4 litre (47 fl oz) baking dish with butter and add two sheets of filo
pastry, brushing each layer with butter. Top with another two sheets of pastry,
but place them in the opposite direction, also brushing each layer with butter.
Repeat this process with four more sheets of pastry. Spoon the cheese filling
over the pastry and fold in the edges. Brush the remaining pastry sheets with
butter, then use them to fill the gaps and cover the cheese filling, scrunching
them up to create ruffles on top.

Scatter the top of the tiropita with the sesame seeds and bake for
30–35 minutes, until the pastry is golden brown and crisp.

Cut the tiropita into six pieces and serve with lemon wedges.

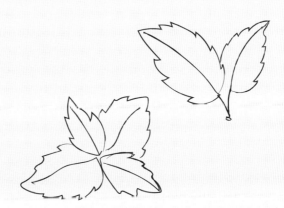

'Kaliméra' rizogalo

GREEK RICE PUDDING WITH CHERRIES

1.4 litres (47 fl oz) full-cream (whole) milk

55 g (¼ cup) caster (superfine) sugar

1 teaspoon vanilla bean paste

1 lemon, zested into wide strips

200 g (1 cup) medium-grain rice

2 egg yolks

1 teaspoon cornflour (corn starch)

Greek sour cherries in syrup, to serve

~~~~~~

PREP IS YOUR BEST FRIEND:

If serving hot, rizogalo is best served as soon as it's ready, but if you are short on time, you can make it an hour before your guests arrive and reheat over low heat, with a little extra milk to loosen it slightly. Be careful to not overcook, as the rice will turn gluggy.

PERFECTLY PAIRED WITH:

Fruit salad with mojito dressing (see page 54).

We remember Mum making us traditional rizogalo, with a generous sprinkling of cinnamon, for us to take to school. We enjoy it hot and cold, but if you are making rizogalo on a summer's day, place it into the fridge for a couple of hours before serving, then serve with the cherries on top. If the weather is cold, serve it warm for the perfect winter morning meal – creamy luscious rice, scented with lemon and finished with syrupy sour cherries – it is what morning dreams are made of.

You can purchase sour cherries from Greek supermarkets, but if you can't find them, cherry jam will also work well. This recipe serves four, but depending on what other dishes you are serving it with, it could feed six to eight people.

Pour the milk into a deep saucepan over medium heat. Add the sugar, vanilla bean paste and lemon strips and bring to a simmer. Reduce the heat to low and gradually stir in the rice. Simmer, stirring occasionally, for 20 minutes or until creamy.

In a bowl, whisk together the egg yolks and cornflour. Carefully remove 60 ml (¼ cup) of the milk from the pan and add it to the egg yolk mixture, whisking to combine. Pour the egg yolk mixture into the pan and stir well to combine. Continue to cook, stirring occasionally, for a further 10 minutes or until the rice is cooked through and creamy.

To serve, ladle the hot rizogalo into serving glasses or bowls and spoon over a few sour cherries and some syrup from the jar.

Any leftover rizogalo will keep, covered, in the fridge for 2–4 days.

Tsoureki

GREEK EASTER BREAD

3 × 7 g sachets (¾ oz) active dried yeast

125 ml (½ cup) full-cream (whole) lukewarm milk

2 tablespoons caster (superfine) sugar

2 tablespoons honey

2 egg yolks, plus 2 whole eggs

50 g (1¾ oz) unsalted butter, melted and cooled

335 g (2¼ cups) plain (all-purpose) flour, sifted, plus extra for dusting

½ teaspoon ground mastiha

1 teaspoon ground mahlepi

1 teaspoon vanilla powder

1 teaspoon salt flakes

½ teaspoon sesame seeds

softened butter and apricot jam, to serve

~~~~~~

PREP IS YOUR BEST FRIEND:
Bake the tsoureki the day before. Make sure it is completely cool before storing in an airtight container.

PERFECTLY PAIRED WITH:
Freddo cappuccino (see page 193).

Tsoureki is a brioche-style bread studded with spices such as mahlepi and mastiha. For us, Greek Easter has always been our favourite celebration, our godparents live across the road from our local Greek church and they have been hosting dinners for the last 30 years. As children, staying up past 12 am was an event we would look forward to, as well as catching up with friends we only saw once or twice a year. As we became older, Greek Easter turned into a fashion parade.

Mahlepi is a unique Greek spice, made from the inner kernels of cherries that are ground into a sandy white powder. It tastes like cherries with a hit of almonds and a floral hint of rose. Mastiha is a resin secreted from the skinos tree in Chios. Most Greek delis sell both ingredients.

Any leftover tsoureki can be sliced, then wrapped in baking paper and placed in a zip-lock bag in the freezer for three months. Simply defrost and toast individual slices, and serve with plenty of butter and apricot jam. If you don't want to freeze the leftover slices, make a bread and butter pudding.

Combine the yeast, milk and half the sugar in a jug, stir and set aside for 10 minutes or until frothy.

In the bowl of a stand mixer with the dough hook attached, combine the yeast mixture, remaining sugar, honey, egg yolks, one whole egg and the butter, and mix on low speed to combine. Add the flour, mastiha, mahlepi, vanilla powder and salt flakes and knead for 10 minutes or until the dough is smooth and elastic and doesn't stick to the bowl (the dough itself will be a little sticky).

Cover the bowl with a clean tea towel and set aside in a warm place for 1 hour to prove or until the dough has doubled in size.

Knock back the dough, then turn out onto a floured work surface and knead for 5 minutes. Divide the dough into three equal portions, then roll into balls.

Start by stretching each dough ball into a 40 cm (16 in) rope. Braid the three ropes of dough together and pinch the ends to seal. Place the tsoureki on a large baking tray lined with baking paper and place in a warm spot again to prove for 1 hour or until risen.

Preheat the oven to 160°C (320°F).

Lightly beat the remaining egg. Brush the tsoureki with the egg wash and scatter with the sesame seeds. Transfer to the oven and bake for 30–35 minutes, until golden brown.

Allow the tsoureki to cool completely, then cut into 2 cm (¾ in) thick slices. Spread with butter and apricot jam and serve.

Cinnamon crepes with honey–butter peaches

250 ml (1 cup) full-cream (whole) milk

2 large eggs

1 teaspoon vanilla bean paste

150 g (1 cup) plain (all-purpose) flour, sifted

1 teaspoon ground cinnamon

2 tablespoons unsalted butter, melted

250 ml (1 cup) pure cream

HONEY-BUTTER PEACHES

4 peaches, sliced into thin wedges

90 g (¼ cup) honey

50 g (1¾ oz) unsalted butter, roughly chopped

~~~~~~

PREP IS YOUR BEST FRIEND:

The crepes can be made before guests arrive and wrapped in a clean tea towel. Simply reheat in the microwave for 2 minutes or in a low oven for 5 minutes.

PERFECTLY PAIRED WITH:

A hot cup of mountain tea.

At Fourka beach on a hot summer's night, a crepe stuffed with Nutella and crushed biscuits is the ultimate late-night treat. Or sometimes a savoury crepe is the perfect pre-dinner meal before hitting the nightclubs. Our favourite combo is ham, cheese and red bell peppers (capsicums).

In Greece, you know summer has arrived when the peaches are sweet and juicy. Laying on a beach bed while listening to the waves and licking the peach juices from your arm ... this is living. If peaches are not in season, use apples instead.

Place the milk, eggs and vanilla in a large bowl and whisk to combine. Add the flour and cinnamon and whisk until smooth.

Drizzle a large non-stick frying pan with a little of the melted butter over medium heat. Pour 60 ml (¼ cup) of the batter into the frying pan and rotate the pan to cover the base with the batter. Cook the crepe for 2 minutes each side or until lightly golden brown, then transfer to a plate and cover to keep warm. Continue with the remaining butter and batter to make eight crepes.

Meanwhile, to make the honey-butter peaches, place the peach in a large frying pan over medium heat, add the honey and butter and cook, stirring occasionally, for 8–10 minutes, until the peach is soft and caramelised, but still holding its shape.

In a large bowl and using electric beaters, whisk the cream to firm peaks.

To serve, add a few tablespoons of cream to each crepe, top with the honey-butter peaches, then fold up and serve.

Lemon thyme psomí

7 g sachet (2¼ teaspoons) active
    dried yeast

2 teaspoons caster (superfine) sugar

500 ml (2 cups) lukewarm water

550 g (1 lb 3 oz) strong bread flour, sifted

40 g (1½ oz) graviera cheese, finely
    grated

1 tablespoon lemon thyme leaves, plus
    extra for scattering

1 teaspoon salt flakes, plus extra
    for sprinkling

2 tablespoons Confit garlic oil
    (see page 210)

1 small lemon, finely sliced

~~~~~~~

PREP IS YOUR BEST FRIEND:

Our psomí is best eaten fresh from the
oven, but if time is an issue the bread can
be baked the night before, then covered
tightly with plastic wrap and left at room
temperature. Preheat the oven to 180°C
(350°F), spray the bread with some
water (this helps the bread get back to
being super fluffy and soft) and bake for
15 minutes or until the bread is crispy.
Weighing out your dry ingredients
the night before can also save you time.

PERFECTLY PAIRED WITH:

Any of our mezze and big plates.

Yiayia would ask us daily: 'théleis lígo psomí?' (do you want some bread?).
Eating freshly baked bread, sitting in front of the heater and watching
Days of Our Lives with Yiayia is a memory that is still very vivid for us.
    Our psomí is very similar to a focaccia, with a fluffy and light texture.

Place the yeast, sugar and lukewarm water in a bowl and set aside for 5 minutes
or until frothy.

Place the flour, cheese, thyme and salt flakes in the bowl of a stand mixer with
the dough hook attached. Pour in the yeast mixture, along with 1 tablespoon
of the confit garlic oil, and knead on low speed for 10 minutes or until a smooth
sticky dough forms.

Transfer the dough to a lightly greased bowl and cover with a damp tea towel.
Set aside at room temperature for 1 hour or until doubled in size.

Preheat the oven to 200°C (400°F). Grease and line the base and sides of
a 30 cm × 20 cm × 4 cm (12 in × 8 in × 1½ in) baking tray with baking paper.

Transfer the dough to the prepared tray, then use your fingers to push out the
dough to fill the tray. Set aside for 30 minutes or until risen slightly. Drizzle
the remaining confit garlic oil over the dough and press your fingers into the
dough to form dimples (just like a focaccia).

Transfer the psomí to the oven and bake for 40 minutes. Halfway through
cooking, carefully lay the lemon slices on top of the psomí and scatter with
extra lemon thyme and a few salt flakes. Continue to bake for the remaining
time until golden. Serve the psomí warm.

Greek-style baked beans

80 ml (⅓ cup) extra virgin olive oil

1 white onion, finely sliced

3 teaspoons mashed Jammy garlic (see page 207)

2 teaspoons honey

salt flakes and freshly cracked black pepper

½ bunch oregano, leaves picked and chopped, plus extra leaves to serve

450 g (1 lb) tomatoes, chopped

2 × 400 g (14 oz) tins butter (lima) beans, drained and rinsed

~~~~~

PREP IS YOUR BEST FRIEND:

The beans can be made the day before – cool completely before storing in an airtight container. To reheat, place the beans in a saucepan over low heat for 10 minutes, stirring constantly to avoid overcooking the beans.

PERFECTLY PAIRED WITH:

Our Lemon thyme psomí (see page 42).

There is a cheat's version and a slow version of our Greek-style baked beans. Here, we've given you our cheat's option, so you have some extra time on your hands. The slow version involves soaking the beans overnight and boiling them until cooked. We have used butter beans in this recipe but you can use cannellini beans as well.

Leftover beans can be eaten during the week and served on top of our toasted lemon thyme psomí. Our beans are also a great mezze, served cold in a small dish drizzled with extra virgin olive oil and some lemon wedges.

Heat the olive oil in a large saucepan over low heat. Add the onion, jammy garlic and honey, season with salt flakes and cracked black pepper and cook, stirring frequently, for 15 minutes or until the onion is soft and jammy.

Increase the heat to medium, add the oregano and tomato and cook for a further 10 minutes. Stir through the beans and heat through for a further 5 minutes.

Serve the beans topped with extra oregano leaves.

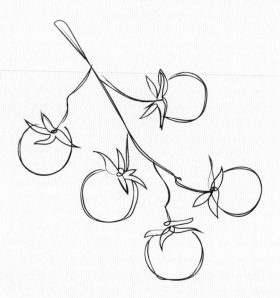

Cheesy truffle pitas

100 g (3½ oz) haloumi

100 g (3½ oz) kefalotyri

100 g (3½ oz) Greek feta, crumbled

20 g (¾ oz) finely grated black truffle

1 tablespoon extra virgin olive oil

8 medium Greek pita breads

~~~~~~~

PERFECTLY PAIRED WITH:

A cup of hot coffee.

✻Fancy pants alert.✻ When truffles are in season, we suggest buying a small amount and treating yourself and your favourite people. We've used 20 g (¾ oz) of fresh truffle here, but you can also use truffle paste. If using the latter, spread a teaspoon of paste onto each pita bread, then top with the cheese mixture.

Grate the haloumi and kefalotyri into a bowl and stir through the feta and truffle.

Heat 1 teaspoon of the olive oil in a large non-stick frying pan over medium heat. Place a pita bread in the pan, scatter with one-quarter of the cheese mixture and top with another pita bread. Fry the pita breads for 2–3 minutes each side, until lightly golden and the cheese is melted. Repeat with remaining ingredients to make four truffle pitas.

Serve the truffle pitas immediately, cut into triangles.

Bougatsa

CRISPY FILO CUSTARD PIE

125 g (4⅓ oz) caster (superfine) sugar

3 eggs

2 teaspoons orange juice

125 g (1 cup) fine semolina

500 ml (2 cups) full-cream (whole) milk

200 ml (7 fl oz) melted butter

8 sheets filo pastry

ground cinnamon, for dusting

icing sugar, for dusting

~~~~~~

PREP IS YOUR BEST FRIEND:
You can prepare the bougatsa the night before – simply cover with plastic wrap and place in the fridge.

PERFECTLY PAIRED WITH:
Freddo cappuccino (see page 193).

Northern Greece is famous for its bougatsa and we think the best can be found in Thessaloniki. Every year we visit, we make sure we try a new spot and our list inevitably grows. Layers of buttery filo pastry with a sweet creamy semolina custard, dusted with icing sugar and cinnamon, is the perfect morning treat.

We have baked our version in a baking tin, which is perfect for entertaining. Traditionally, bougatsa is served chopped into small squares.

Preheat the oven to 180°C (350°F). Lightly grease a 24 cm × 29 cm × 2.5 cm (9½ in × 11½ in × 1 in) baking tin.

Place the sugar and eggs in the bowl of a stand mixer with the whisk attached and beat on high speed for 4–5 minutes, until thick and fluffy. Add the orange juice, semolina and milk and whisk for 2–3 minutes, until combined.

Transfer the semolina mixture to a large saucepan over low heat and cook, stirring constantly, for 10 minutes or until the mixture has thickened slightly. Pour in half the melted butter and mix to combine. Allow to cool slightly.

Lay one sheet of filo pastry over the base of the prepared tin and brush with a little of the remaining butter. Repeat with five more pastry sheets. Pour the custard over the layered pastry and top with the remaining two sheets of filo pastry, brushing with butter in between. Brush the top with butter and bake for 30 minutes or until lightly golden and crispy.

Dust the bougatsa with cinnamon and icing sugar and slice into six pieces to serve.

Tomato tart

225 g (1½ cups) plain (all-purpose) flour, sifted

130 g (4½ oz) chilled unsalted butter, chopped

salt flakes

60 ml (¼ cup) chilled water

180 g (6½ oz) galotyri cheese

300 g (10½ oz) mixed heirloom tomatoes, cut into 5 mm (¼ in) thick slices

3 sprigs thyme, leaves picked, plus extra leaves to serve

1 egg, lightly beaten

40 g (1½ oz) graviera cheese, finely grated

8 anchovy fillets in oil (optional)

~~~~~~~

PREP IS YOUR BEST FRIEND:

The pastry can be made the day before and stored in the fridge. Remove the pastry 15 minutes before rolling out.

PERFECTLY PAIRED WITH:

For a lunch spread, serve the tomato tart with our Iceberg and graviera salad with tarragon buttermilk dressing (see page 134).

We remember our first holiday to Greece back in 1996. It was our first overseas trip with Mum and we arrived at Yiayia's village where everyone was there to greet us. Mum's aunt Aleka handed us a tomato from her garden and from that moment we knew what a tomato should taste like.

This tart can be served any time of the day, which makes it a great recipe to have on hand. Don't be intimidated by making your own pastry, we promise you it's a simple dough to work with and isn't hard to handle.

Place the flour, butter and 1 teaspoon of salt flakes in a food processor and process until the mixture resembles fine breadcrumbs. With the motor running, add the chilled water and process until a smooth dough forms. Wrap the dough in plastic wrap and set aside in the fridge to chill for 30 minutes.

Preheat the oven to 200°C (400°F).

Roll the dough out between two sheets of baking paper to a 35 cm (14 in) circle. Return to the fridge for 15 minutes to rest.

Place the pastry on a large baking tray and remove the top sheet of baking paper. Spread the galotyri over the pastry leaving a 5 cm (2 in) border and top with the tomato slices. Season with salt flakes and scatter with the thyme leaves. Fold the pastry edge over the filling to secure it, then brush the pastry with the beaten egg. Bake for 30 minutes or until the pastry is lightly golden and crisp.

Remove the tart from the oven and scatter with graviera cheese, then cook for a further 15 minutes or until the cheese is melted.

Serve the tart, topped with the anchovy fillets (if using) and extra thyme leaves.

Green olive & mortadella loaf

1 teaspoon extra virgin olive oil, plus extra for brushing

150 g (5½ oz) thickly sliced mortadella, roughly chopped

375 g (2½ cups) plain (all-purpose) flour, sifted, plus extra for dusting

1 tablespoon caster (superfine) sugar

7 g sachet (2¼ teaspoons) active dried yeast

80 g (2¾ oz) pitted green olives in brine, drained and chopped

handful of oregano leaves, torn

1 teaspoon salt flakes

100 g (3½ oz) unsalted butter, softened, plus extra for greasing and to serve

180 ml (6 fl oz) full-cream (whole) milk

1 egg

~~~~~~~

PREP IS YOUR BEST FRIEND:

The bread can be baked a couple of hours before guests arrive or baked the day before and reheated in a 150°C (300°F) oven for 20 minutes.

PERFECTLY PAIRED WITH:

Serve with our Greek-style baked beans (see page 44) for a lovely breakfast option. Or serve for lunch or dinner with our Roasted garlic and fennel tzatziki (see page 62) and Whipped feta, chargrilled piperiés and almonds (see page 64).

When we think of mortadella, we have a little giggle. As children we used to think it was made with horse meat. We are not sure why and who made us believe this. Anyway, great news, mortadella is not made from horse meat, but with pork and pork fat. It is made by mincing the pork into a smooth paste and studding it with pork fat pieces, before being placed in a casing and steamed.

Yiayia would buy Papou shaved mortadella every week from the deli and he loved it with his olives, fresh bread and a bottle of dark pale ale.

Heat the olive oil in a frying pan over medium heat, add the mortadella and cook for 5–7 minutes, until crisp and golden brown. Transfer to a plate lined with paper towel to drain and cool.

Place the flour, sugar, yeast, olives, oregano leaves, cooled mortadella and salt flakes in the bowl of a stand mixer with the dough hook attached and briefly mix to combine.

Melt the butter in a small saucepan over medium–low heat, add the milk and warm through for about 2 minutes. Remove from the heat and allow to cool slightly, then whisk in the egg.

With the stand mixer on medium speed, gradually add the egg mixture to the flour mixture and knead until just combined. Increase the speed to medium–high and knead for 8 minutes or until the dough is smooth. Transfer the dough to a lightly greased bowl, cover with a clean tea towel and stand in a warm place for 45–60 minutes, until doubled in size.

Knock back the dough and turn out onto a floured work surface. Shape the dough into a round ball, then carefully transfer to a large sheet of baking paper and lift into a 24 cm (9½ in) round cast-iron casserole dish (Dutch oven). Cover with a damp tea towel and stand in a warm place for 30 minutes or until risen slightly.

Meanwhile, preheat the oven to 180°C (350°F).

Brush the top of the dough with oil and bake for 40–45 minutes, until the loaf is golden and sounds hollow when tapped. Turn out onto a wire rack to cool.

Slice and serve with butter.

Fruit salad with mojito dressing

1 kg (2 lb 3 oz) watermelon, cut into
    wedges

500 g (1 lb 2 oz) honeydew melon,
    peeled and cut into chunks

200 g (7 oz) red and white seedless
    grapes

Greek-style yoghurt and honey, to serve

MOJITO DRESSING

2 tablespoons caster (superfine) sugar

10 g (½ cup) mint leaves

1 teaspoon spiced rum (optional; omit
    for a booze-free brunch)

juice of 3 limes

Rum for breakfast might seem a little extreme, but it is optional and you won't really taste the small amount used here. Mojitos are nostalgic for us, they take us back to our Greek summers drinking at the beach bars until the sun set.

We have used summer fruits here, but please substitute with whatever fruits are in season. The mojito dressing is also delicious served as a drink mixed with soda water and ice.

For the mojito dressing, place the ingredients in a food processor and process until the mint is finely chopped.

Place the fruit on a serving platter and drizzle with the mojito dressing. Serve alongside Greek-style yoghurt and honey.

PREP IS YOUR BEST FRIEND:
The mojito dressing can be made the day before and stored in a jar with a lid.

PERFECTLY PAIRED WITH:
The salad can be served alongside our Tahini pancakes with yoghurt and orange (see page 26).

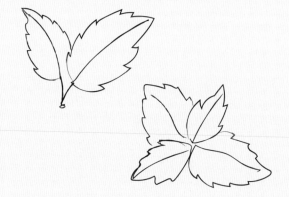

Mushroom & horta ruffled pie

⅓ bunch leaf chicory

375 g (13 oz) brown mushrooms, sliced

1 tablespoon olive oil

salt flakes and freshly cracked
    black pepper

½ bunch parsley, leaves picked
    and chopped

200 ml (7 fl oz) pure cream

100 ml (3½ fl oz) full-cream (whole) milk

3 eggs

10 sheets filo pastry

100 g (3½ oz) butter, melted

450 g (1 lb) fresh ricotta

~~~~~~~~

PREP IS YOUR BEST FRIEND:

We suggest making this pie fresh as
it tastes best straight from the oven.
The mushrooms and leaf chicory can
be prepared the day before, adding
the parsley leaves just before cooking.

PERFECTLY PAIRED WITH:

As a lunch or dinner option, serve
alongside our Roasted garlic and fennel
tzatziki (see page 62) and our OG
Greek saláta (see page 133).

A pie has to be one of the cosiest dishes, the smell and taste make you want
to be around the table with family. You will find several pie recipes in this
book, from bougatsa and kotopita, to tiropita and galaktoboureko ... Yes, we
are pie obsessed.

We have used leaf chicory for our horta (greens), and for this recipe
you will need about half a small bunch. Thanks to Jim Fuller who we met at
a mushroom foraging day and taught us how to cook mushrooms properly.
It's crazy to think we have been doing it wrong all these years. Jim's method
helps keep the mushroom flavour intact by cooking mushrooms in water.
No matter how much water you add to the pan, the mushrooms won't get soggy.

Preheat the oven to 200°C (400°F). Grease a 3 litre (3 qt) round baking tin.

Blanch the leaf chicory in a saucepan of salted boiling water for 5 minutes,
then drain, making sure to remove any excess water. Set aside to cool, then
roughly chop.

Place the mushroom and 250 ml (1 cup) of water in a large frying pan
over medium–high heat and simmer for 15 minutes or until the water has
evaporated. Add the olive oil and fry the mushroom for 5 minutes or until
golden brown. Season with salt flakes and cracked black pepper, then
remove from the heat and allow to cool slightly. Stir through the parsley
and leaf chicory.

In a large bowl, whisk the cream, milk and eggs until combined. Set aside.

Lay one sheet of filo pastry on a chopping board and brush with a little of
the melted butter. Scatter with 45 g (1½ oz) of the ricotta and 2 tablespoons
of the mushroom mixture. Starting at the bottom of the filo sheet, concertina
the pastry away from you, until you have a folded pastry strip. Place the strip
in the centre of the prepared tin, then coil the pastry into a snail shape.
Repeat with the remaining ingredients, adding to the snail shape, until you
have filled the tin.

Transfer the pie to the oven and bake for 40 minutes.

Reduce the oven temperature to 180°C (350°F) and evenly pour the cream
mixture over the crispy pastry. Cook for a further 20 minutes or until the
custard is set and golden brown. Slice and serve.

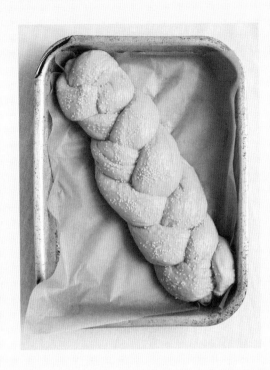

MEZZE

CHAPTER
02

MEZÉDES

We think that without mezédes, there is no real start to a party.
Hot or cold mezze get the taste buds rolling and, of course, leave a very
good first impression. Most of the time our last-minute dinner parties
consist of just mezze; they are quick to put together and very little work
is required to get them on the table. We love using up what's in the
fridge to create these small dishes – any tired-looking vegetables can
be roasted and blitzed into something creamy and topped with roasted
seeds. Keeping packets of pita bread in the freezer also makes things
easier if you don't have time to make your own – simply combine a little
oil with our Greek spice mix on page 206 and brush over pita breads
before putting straight into a hot frying pan.

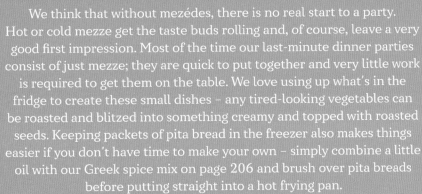

In this chapter, we have included recipes that you will want to make
again and again. The joy of dips means you can prepare them at
any time and store in the fridge for a few days. Then if guests arrive
unexpectedly on your doorstep you have something delicious ready
to serve. In Greece, mezédes are the secret to long lunches and
dinners – the Greeks will graze for hours, picking away slowly with
sips of tsipouro in between. That is the Greek life.

Our mezédes are stress free and simple to whip up. We know how time
can be limited with so much going on in our lives, so these recipes are
enjoyable to make but also quick to put together.

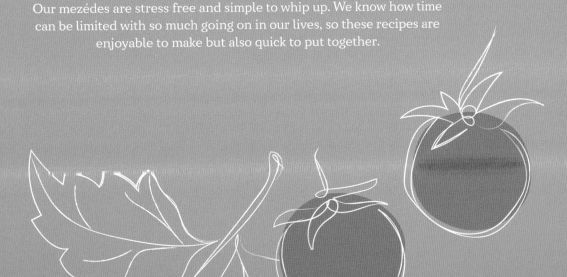

Roasted garlic & fennel tzatziki

1 small garlic bulb

80 ml (⅓ cup) extra virgin olive oil,
   plus 2 tablespoons extra

500 g (2 cups) Greek-style yoghurt

1 small fennel bulb, finely chopped,
   fronds reserved

½ bunch mint, leaves picked and
   finely chopped

½ bunch dill, fronds picked and
   finely chopped

juice of 1 lemon

1 teaspoon salt flakes

~~~~~~

PREP IS YOUR BEST FRIEND:
The tzatziki can be made the day before
and kept in an airtight container in
the fridge. Stir well just before serving.

PERFECTLY PAIRED WITH:
Scoop our Oregano yoghurt pita bread
(see page 78) straight into the tzatziki.

No Greek feast is complete without a bowl of tzatziki. It is the quintessential
Greek dip, with garlic, thick yoghurt and a good amount of lemon. Our version
includes crunchy fennel, which is not traditional, but we promise it will open
a new pathway you didn't know existed.

For the creamiest, thickest yoghurt, strain it overnight in the fridge in a
square of muslin (cheesecloth) hung over a bowl to catch the whey. And, of
course, if you don't like fennel, you can use the more traditional cucumber
instead. Simply grate two small cucumbers and squeeze out the excess liquid
before adding to the yoghurt.

Preheat the oven to 180°C (350°F).

Using a sharp knife, slice the very top off the garlic, just enough to expose
the garlic cloves. Place the garlic bulb on a piece of foil and drizzle with
1 tablespoon of the extra oil. Wrap the garlic tightly in the foil and roast
for 45 minutes or until the garlic is jammy. Allow the garlic to cool slightly,
then squeeze the roasted cloves into a large bowl.

Add the yoghurt, the 80 ml (⅓ cup) of olive oil, fennel, herbs, lemon juice and
salt flakes to the roasted garlic and mix until completely combined.

To serve the tzatziki, spoon into a serving bowl or onto a plate and top with the
reserved fennel fronds and remaining tablespoon of oil.

Leftover tzatziki will keep in an airtight container in the fridge for up to 5 days.

Whipped feta, chargrilled piperiés & almonds

A FEAST FOR 4

250 g (9 oz) Greek feta, roughly chopped

180 g (6½ oz) Greek-style yoghurt

150 g (5½ oz) Roasted red piperiés (see page 211) or store-bought roasted red bell peppers (capsicums), finely sliced into strips

35 g (¼ cup) roasted almonds, roughly chopped

1 tablespoon extra virgin olive oil

~~~~~~

PREP IS YOUR BEST FRIEND:

The whipped feta and piperiés can be made the day before and stored in the fridge. You can also roast the almonds ahead of time and pop them in a jar until ready to serve. Leftover whipped feta will keep in an airtight container in the fridge for up to 1 week. Spread over sourdough and top with poached eggs, or stir through pasta.

PERFECTLY PAIRED WITH:

Dip in with our Oregano yoghurt pita bread (see page 78) and Tomatokeftedes (see page 76).

There is always a dip or two on our table, no matter what type of gathering we are having. Here, Greek-style yoghurt provides a creamy and smooth base for tangy, salty and crumbly feta, which, once combined, creates a dreamy bowl of goodness that pairs perfectly with the smoky peppers and roasted almonds.

Very little work is required to make the whipped feta and it looks effortlessly stunning on the table. Sometimes we add a handful of chopped dill fronds to garnish.

In a food processor, pulse the feta and yoghurt for 1–2 minutes, until smooth. Take care not to overwhip the mixture or it will become too runny.

To serve, spoon the whipped feta into a shallow serving bowl, top with the sliced piperiés and chopped almonds, and drizzle with the oil.

Haloumi with honey–roasted tomatoes

600 g (1 lb 5 oz) cherry tomatoes
   on the vine

½ bunch oregano, leaves picked

2 tablespoons honey

80 ml (⅓ cup) extra virgin olive oil

1 tablespoon red wine vinegar

salt flakes

2 × 250 g (9 oz) flat blocks haloumi, sliced
   horizontally through the middle

½ teaspoon dried oregano

~~~~~~~~

PREP IS YOUR BEST FRIEND:

If time is tight, roast the tomatoes a
couple of hours before serving and keep
them at room temperature. Haloumi
is best pan-fried immediately before
serving – if left to sit for too long, it
will go hard and the texture will be
unpleasant.

PERFECTLY PAIRED WITH:

Lemon thyme psomí (see page 42) to soak
up all of the sweet tomato juices.

This is the number-one requested cheese from our non-Greek friends and
we don't blame them. Haloumi is made from goat and sheep's milk, with
a tangy and salty flavour, and is best cooked in a hot pan to give you a nice
charred flavour. Pairing the cheese with sweet, jammy, roasted tomatoes
is a combination that will have everyone coming back for more. You can
choose a variety of small and large tomatoes for prettiness, or just use cherry
tomatoes, as we have done here, as they are sweeter and more flavoursome.

You can put this dish together super quickly – the tomatoes can be thrown
in the oven just before your guests arrive, which gives you enough time to
quickly jump in the shower and get ready. The haloumi can be fried once
everyone is chatting away.

Preheat the oven to 200°C (400°F).

Place the tomatoes in a large roasting tin and scatter with the oregano leaves.
Drizzle over the honey, 2 tablespoons of the olive oil and the vinegar, and
season with salt flakes. Roast for 30 minutes or until the tomatoes are blistered
and jammy. Set aside.

Pat dry the haloumi with paper towel, to remove the excess liquid.

Heat the remaining oil in a large non-stick frying pan over medium–high heat,
add the haloumi and cook for 2–3 minutes each side, until golden brown.

To serve, place the haloumi in the roasting tin with the tomatoes and sprinkle
with the dried oregano. Serve with plenty of fresh bread to soak up all of the
beautiful juices.

Taramasalata

100 g (3½ oz) tarama caviar

1 teaspoon mashed Jammy garlic
(see page 207) or 1 garlic clove,
crushed

70 g (2½ oz) stale white bread, crusts
removed and torn

250 ml (1 cup) extra virgin olive oil,
plus extra to serve

6 small ice cubes

juice of 1 lemon

salt flakes

salmon caviar, to serve (optional)

~~~~~~

PREP IS YOUR BEST FRIEND:
The tarama can be made the day before
and stored in an airtight container in the
fridge. The flavour will actually improve.
Give it a good stir before spooning onto
the serving plate.

PERFECTLY PAIRED WITH:
Lemon thyme psomí (see page 42), or
for an extra dipping sauce, the tarama is
also lovely with our Snapper croquettes
with lemon and fried caper mayonnaise
(see page 90).

There are two types of tarama: the widely consumed pink version sold in
tubs at the supermarket, which has a subtle fish flavour and uses potato; and
white tarama, which has a stronger fish flavour and is made using soaked stale
bread. Once you try the latter, we guarantee you will never go back. You will
find tarama caviar at fishmongers and specialty stores – it's usually made with
mullet roe that has been blended into a paste. The salmon caviar in this recipe
is optional, so no pressure to buy it, but it really adds a delicious salty pop.

In case you're wondering what the ice cubes do, they help give the tarama
a light and fluffy texture.

Place the tarama caviar and garlic in a food processor and process until
smooth. Place the bread in a small bowl and cover with water, then drain
and squeeze out the excess water. Add the bread to the food processor and
continue to process until smooth. With the motor running, gradually add
the olive oil in a slow, steady stream until the mixture emulsifies. Add the ice
cubes, one by one, and process until completely blended and silky and smooth.
Add the lemon juice, season with salt flakes and mix to combine.

To serve, spoon the tamara onto a serving plate, top with salmon caviar
(if using) and drizzle with extra oil.

Orange & chilli-marinated olives

650 g (1 lb 7 oz) mixed olives

1 long red chilli, finely sliced

3 garlic cloves

2 teaspoons fennel seeds

3 sprigs rosemary

1 large orange, zested into strips

1 large lemon, zested into strips

80 ml (⅓ cup) extra virgin olive oil

~~~~~~

PREP IS YOUR BEST FRIEND:
This is an easy make-ahead mezze.
Simply combine the ingredients the night
before and remove from the fridge
2 hours before roasting. Place in the oven
just before guests arrive, so you can greet
them with warm olives and your house
smelling just like a Greek taverna.

PERFECTLY PAIRED WITH:
We are obsessed with olives, so go ahead
and serve them with most of our recipes.

If there is one mezze you need on your table, it's warm olives – no Greek feast
is complete without them! Usually we make a double batch and bake half the
quantity for guests and save the rest to snack on during the week when we
forget to prepare dinner or come home from an event and need a pre-bedtime
bite. The chilli can be omitted, but it adds a subtle heat that works perfectly
with the citrus.

Preheat the oven to 200°C (400°F).

Place the ingredients in a baking dish and stir to combine. Transfer to the oven
and roast, stirring halfway through cooking, for 20 minutes or until the olives
are warm and fragrant.

Serve warm.

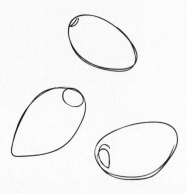

Fava with pickled grapes & caperberries

330 g (1½ cups) yellow split peas

80 ml (⅓ cup) extra virgin olive oil

1 small red onion, finely chopped

2 garlic cloves, finely sliced

600 ml (20½ fl oz) vegetable stock

1 bay leaf

40 g (¼ cup) caperberries, drained and cut in half

2 tablespoons dill fronds, finely chopped

pita breads, to serve

PICKLED GRAPES

150 g (5½ oz) seedless black or red grapes, cut in half

60 ml (¼ cup) red wine vinegar

1 teaspoon caster (superfine) sugar

~~~~~

PREP IS YOUR BEST FRIEND:
The fava can be made the day before – simply cool completely, then store in an airtight container in the fridge. When ready to serve, place the cold fava in a small saucepan over low heat and add 1–2 tablespoons of stock to loosen it slightly. Warm through for about 10 minutes, until the fava is smooth.

PERFECTLY PAIRED WITH:
Chargrilled octopus with Greek salsa verde (see page 128).

To be honest, we were never a fan of fava growing up. We think it was the colour that made us not want to eat it. Now, of course, we love it. To get things straight, fava isn't actually made with fava (broad) beans, it is made with yellow split peas and is one of the most famous recipes to come from Santorini. Traditionally, it is served with sliced raw red onion, so feel free to replace the grapes with onion.

Rinse the yellow split peas under cold running water. Drain well.

For the pickled grapes, place the grapes in a small heatproof bowl. Place the vinegar, sugar and 60 ml (¼ cup) of water in a small saucepan and bring to the boil. Allow to cool slightly, then pour the liquid over the grapes. Set aside to pickle.

Heat 60 ml (¼ cup) of the olive oil in a saucepan over medium heat, add the onion and garlic and cook, stirring occasionally, for 8–10 minutes, until the onion has softened. Add the split peas and continue to cook 4–5 minutes, until slightly toasted. Add the stock and bay leaf, bring to the boil, then reduce the heat to a simmer and cook, skimming off any foam that rises to the surface, for 50–55 minutes, until the split peas are tender and broken down. Discard the bay leaf. Using a stick blender, blend the fava until smooth.

To serve, top the fava with the pickled grapes, caperberries, dill and remaining oil. Serve with pita breads.

Saganaki with fig jam & fried oregano

2 × 400 g (14 oz) blocks kefalograviera

35 g (¼ cup) plain (all-purpose) flour

60 ml (¼ cup) extra virgin olive oil, plus 1 tablespoon extra

½ bunch oregano, leaves picked

160 g (½ cup) fig jam

lemon wedges, to serve

~~~~~~~

PREP IS YOUR BEST FRIEND:
Saganaki is best fried and served straight away. If it sits for too long it will go hard and tough.

PERFECTLY PAIRED WITH:
Grain salad (see page 150) and Pork gyros (see page 122).

Saganaki is a classic dish found on all Greek restaurant menus. Both graviera and kefalograviera cheese are used to make saganaki, as their texture is perfect for frying and achieving the right amount of gooiness. The flour dusting encourages the crispness and golden colour of the cheese, which protects the goodness inside. The timing for serving saganaki is crucial – be sure to serve it as soon as it's fried and enjoy hot. Jam is not only for spreading on toast, and here the sweetness cuts through the strong, rich cheese. We have used fig jam, but cherry jam or apricot jam also work beautifully.

Dip the kefalograviera in a bowl of water, then shake off any excess liquid and dust in the flour, making sure to coat well.

Heat the olive oil in a large non-stick frying pan over medium–high heat, add the kefalograviera and cook for 2–3 minutes each side, until golden. Remove the cheese from the pan and wipe out the frying pan with paper towel. Drizzle with the extra oil and fry the oregano leaves for 30 seconds or until crisp.

Serve the saganaki topped with the fig jam and fried oregano, and with lemon wedges for squeezing over.

Tomatokeftedes

FRIED TOMATO FRITTERS

600 g (1 lb 5 oz) cherry tomatoes,
    roughly chopped

2 small red onions, finely chopped

salt flakes and freshly cracked
    black pepper

50 g (2 cups) mixed herbs, such as dill
    fronds, Greek basil and mint leaves,
    finely chopped

pinch of ground cinnamon

150 g (1 cup) plain (all-purpose) flour,
    sifted

1 teaspoon baking powder

100 g (3½ oz) Greek feta, crumbled

80 ml (⅓ cup) olive oil

oregano leaves, to serve

Santorini is known to grow some of the best tomatoes in Greece, and tomatokeftedes are Santorini's iconic mezze. For this recipe, aim for just-ripe tomatoes that are still holding their shape, and remember that summer tomatoes are always best to use.

Place the tomato and onion in a fine-meshed sieve with a bowl underneath, toss with 1 teaspoon of salt flakes and allow to sit for 30 minutes – this helps the tomato and onion release their liquid. Discard the liquid.

Place the tomato and onion mixture in a bowl and add the herbs, cinnamon, flour, baking powder and feta. Season with salt flakes and cracked black pepper and mix to combine – the mixture should be a little sticky and just hold together. Set aside in the fridge for 30 minutes, so the mixture can soften and slightly set.

Heat the olive oil in a large non-stick frying pan over medium heat. Working in batches, add heaped tablespoons of the tomato mixture to the pan and cook for 4–6 minutes, turning halfway through cooking, until golden and crispy. Remove with a slotted spoon and drain on paper towel.

Scatter the tomatokeftedes with oregano leaves and serve.

PREP IS YOUR BEST FRIEND:
The tomato mixture can be made an hour before guests arrive and set aside in the fridge until ready to fry; alternatively, the fried tomatokeftedes can sit at room temperature before serving.

PERFECTLY PAIRED WITH:
Dip the tomatokeftedes in our Roasted garlic and fennel tzatziki (see page 62).

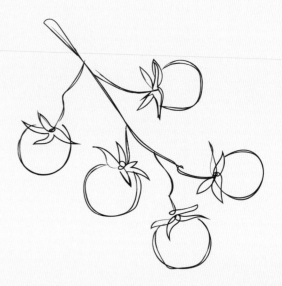

Oregano yoghurt pita breads

500 g (1 lb 2 oz) self raising flour, sifted, plus extra if needed and for dusting

500 g (2 cups) Greek-style yoghurt

1 tablespoon baking powder

1 tablespoon salt flakes

½ bunch oregano, leaves picked and finely chopped

extra virgin olive oil spray

~~~~~~

PREP IS YOUR BEST FRIEND:
You can cook the pita breads the day before and reheat in a low oven, just before guests arrive.

PERFECTLY PAIRED WITH:
Use the pitas for the Pork gyros (see page 122) and, of course, any and all of our dips.

Our mum's aunt, Thea Aleka, dries bunches of oregano in her garage and the smell always transports us back to Yiayia's village. The pepperiness of the herb works beautifully in these Greek pitas, but if oregano is not your favourite herb, you can replace it with rosemary or thyme leaves.

If you are hosting a small dinner party and don't end up cooking all the dough, roll the leftovers into pitas and place a piece of baking paper between each one so they won't stick together, then cover with plastic wrap and refrigerate for the next day. We love frying the pitas for breakfast and topping with a fried egg and some sliced tomatoes. They also make a fantastic quick pizza base.

Place the flour, yoghurt, baking powder, salt flakes and oregano in a large bowl and mix with a wooden spoon until a dough forms. Add a little water if the mixture seems too dry, or more flour if the mixture seems too wet.

Transfer the dough to a clean work surface and dust with a little extra flour. Knead the dough for 3–5 minutes, then divide into 12 equal pieces and roll into small balls.

Dust a rolling pin with flour and roll the balls of dough into 15 cm (6 in) circles.

Place a frying pan over medium heat and spray with olive oil. Working with one pita bread at a time, cook the pitas for 3–4 minutes each side, until lightly charred. Serve hot.

Pork & feta keftedes

GREEK MEATBALLS

500 g (1 lb 2 oz) minced (ground) pork

1 red onion, grated and patted dry to
remove excess liquid

60 g (2 oz) Greek feta, crumbled

handful of parsley, leaves picked and
finely chopped

handful of dill fronds, finely chopped,
plus extra to serve

1 egg, lightly beaten

3 tablespoons plain (all-purpose) flour

3 teaspoons mashed Jammy garlic
(see page 207)

1 tablespoon salt flakes

80 ml (⅓ cup) olive oil

Oregano yoghurt pita breads
(see page 78), to serve

~~~~~

PREP IS YOUR BEST FRIEND:
The meatballs can be rolled the night
before and placed on a tray. Cover well
and refrigerate. The next day, remove
the meatballs from the fridge 20 minutes
before frying. Frying the meatballs an
hour before guests arrive is also fine –
we tend to do this as the kitchen can get
a little smoky and smelly. The meatballs
can sit at room temperature, covered,
ready for when guests arrive.

PERFECTLY PAIRED WITH:
Serve the keftedes with any of our dips.

If we close our eyes and inhale the smell of freshly cooked keftedes, our eyes
start to water. Sizzling meatballs frying away on the stovetop is very nostalgic
for us. Our memories of Yiayia's kitchen are always present; we remember
her squeezing the mince between her fingers, combining the ingredients
and rolling the keftedes into small balls. To this day, we still make them and
instantly feel like we are back home and in that moment with Yiayia.

A great mezze to start a dinner party, these keftedes pair perfectly with
our roasted garlic and fennel tzatziki on page 62, the taramasalata on page
68 and oregano yoghurt pita breads. Leftover keftedes can be mashed up
and added to a frying pan with eggs and grated kasseri cheese for a breakfast
option. We also enjoy cold keftedes.

This is Luke's (Vikki's husband) favourite recipe – he would eat keftedes
every night of the week if he could.

In a large bowl, combine the minced pork, onion, feta, parsley, dill, egg,
2 tablespoons of the flour, the garlic and salt flakes. Mix with your hands
until well combined.

Sprinkle the remaining flour on a plate. Roll 2 tablespoons of the pork mixture
into a meatball, then roll to coat in the flour. Repeat to make 14 keftedes.

Heat the olive oil in a large frying pan over medium heat, add the keftedes
and shallow-fry, turning occasionally, for 10 minutes or until golden brown.

Transfer the keftedes to a serving plate, scatter with dill fronds and serve
with pita breads on the side.

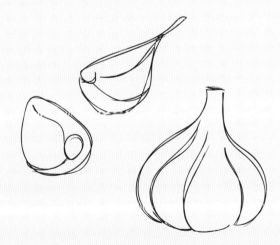

Lamb pita breads

2 teaspoons mashed Jammy garlic
    (see page 207)

700 g (1 lb 9 oz) minced (ground) lamb

½ bunch parsley, leaves picked and
    finely chopped

1 teaspoon dried oregano

½ teaspoon sweet paprika

2 teaspoons dijon mustard

2 teaspoons salt flakes

6 × 18 cm (7 in) pita breads

3 teaspoons extra virgin olive oil

TO SERVE

Greek-style yoghurt

Greek golden pepperoncini

finely sliced red onion

baby cucumbers, halved lengthways

Roasted red piperiés (see page 211)
    or store-bought roasted red bell
    peppers (capsicums)

lemon wedges

This recipe is inspired by Helena's first kitchen job at Salona restaurant in Melbourne, a well-established restaurant known for traditional Greek food. It is an interpretation of what they served as a lunch special, which was one of Helena's favourite dishes. Feel free to substitute the minced lamb for beef, chicken or pork.

Place the garlic, lamb, parsley, oregano, paprika, mustard and salt flakes in a large bowl and use your hands to mix well until combined.

Press 120 g (4½ oz) of the mince mixture onto one pita bread, making sure you spread the mince to the edge. Continue with the remaining mince mixture and pita breads.

Heat ½ teaspoon of the olive oil in a large non-stick frying pan over medium heat, add a pita bread, meat side down, and cook for 4 minutes or until the lamb is cooked and crispy. Flip and cook the other side for 2 minutes. Continue with the remaining oil and lamb pitas.

To serve, invite guests to top their pitas with any or all of the serving suggestions. We love to slather our pitas with Greek-style yoghurt, then top with pepperoncini, onion, cucumber and red piperiés, before squeezing over a wedge of lemon.

~~~~~~

PREP IS YOUR BEST FRIEND:

The mince mixture can be pressed onto the pita breads, then placed one on top of another with a sheet of baking paper between each one, and covered and stored in the fridge for a few hours. The mince filling can be prepped the day before and stored in an airtight container in the fridge, ready to press into the pitas the next day.

PERFECTLY PAIRED WITH:

Replace the Greek-style yoghurt with our Roasted garlic and fennel tzatziki (see page 62).

Ouzo-cured kingfish with lemon oil

100 g (3½ oz) salt flakes

100 g (3½ oz) caster (superfine) sugar

100 ml (3½ fl oz) ouzo

600 g (1 lb 5 oz) sashimi-grade kingfish
fillet, skin removed

1 small lemon, peeled and cut into
segments, flesh finely chopped

60 ml (¼ cup) extra virgin olive oil

~~~~~~

PREP IS YOUR BEST FRIEND:
The lemon oil can be made the day before
and stored in a jar with a lid.

PERFECTLY PAIRED WITH:
Fennel, zucchini flower and mint slaw
with currants (see page 140).

Perfect for summer entertaining, kingfish's rich and oily white flesh is
delicious raw and works so beautifully with our lemon oil. If you like, you
can serve the kingfish on some olive oil crackers.

You need to start this recipe the day before.

Combine the salt, sugar and ouzo in a large bowl. Add the kingfish and turn
to coat in the salt mixture, then cover and chill in the fridge for 12–24 hours.

The next day, combine the lemon and oil in a small bowl. Set aside.

Remove the kingfish from the fridge, rinse off the salt mixture and pat
dry with paper towel. Using a sharp knife, finely slice the kingfish and place
on a serving plate. Drizzle with the lemon oil and serve.

Tuna with tomato & dill yoghurt

200 g (7 oz) Greek-style yoghurt

2 tablespoons dill fronds, finely chopped, plus extra to serve

juice of ½ lemon

salt flakes

300 g (10½ oz) sashimi-grade tuna, diced

100 g (3½ oz) heirloom cherry tomatoes, roughly chopped

1 tablespoon chilli oil, plus extra for drizzling

2 teaspoons toasted sesame seeds

Greek rusk breads, to serve

This dish sounds a little fancy, right? Yes, tuna is not cheap, but buying a small piece like this allows you and your guests to enjoy the perfect mezze. Serving the rusk breads on the side allows your guests to dip in and help themselves. This recipe screams summer on a plate.

Combine the yoghurt, dill and lemon juice in a bowl and season with salt flakes.

In a small bowl, combine the tuna, tomato and chilli oil and season with 1 teaspoon of salt flakes.

To serve, spread the yoghurt mixture onto a plate and top with the tuna mixture. Scatter with the sesame seeds and extra dill fronds, and drizzle with extra chilli oil. Serve with rusk breads.

PREP IS YOUR BEST FRIEND:
This dish is best prepared fresh on the day.

PERFECTLY PAIRED WITH:
We love serving our Ouzo-cured kingfish with lemon oil (see page 84) next to this tuna, with a glass of orange wine on a warm afternoon.

Snapper croquettes with lemon & fried caper mayonnaise

400 g (14 oz) desiree potatoes, peeled and roughly chopped

2 tablespoons unsalted butter, softened

200 g (7 oz) skinless snapper fillets, pin-boned and finely chopped

½ bunch dill fronds, finely chopped

small handful of parsley leaves, finely chopped

½ teaspoon fennel seeds, toasted

zest of 1 lemon, plus lemon wedges to serve

salt flakes and freshly cracked black pepper

35 g (¼ cup) plain (all-purpose) flour

2 eggs, lightly beaten

120 g (1½ cups) sourdough breadcrumbs

vegetable oil, for deep-frying

LEMON AND FRIED CAPER MAYONNAISE

200 g (7 oz) whole egg mayonnaise

zest and juice of 1 lemon

1 tablespoon capers, drained, rinsed and chopped, plus 1 tablespoon whole capers

Dad owned a boat when we were young, and every weekend he would bring home buckets of fish. We remember him sitting outside, shirtless, gutting them one by one. These snapper croquettes are in memory of Dad – we know he would have loved them.

Place the potato in a large saucepan of salted water, bring to the boil and cook for 15–20 minutes, until tender. Drain and roughly mash the potato, then add the butter, snapper, herbs, fennel seeds and lemon zest and mix to combine. Season with salt flakes and cracked black pepper.

Place the flour in a bowl and season with salt flakes. Place the beaten egg and breadcrumbs in separate bowls. Roll 2 tablespoons of the croquette mixture into a 4 cm (1½ in) long log, then roll in the flour to coat, followed by the egg and finally the breadcrumbs. Place the croquette on a plate and repeat with the remaining mixture to make 14 croquettes. Chill the croquettes in the fridge for 15 minutes.

For the lemon and fried caper mayonnaise, combine the mayonnaise, lemon zest and juice and the chopped capers in a bowl.

Half-fill a saucepan with vegetable oil and heat to 180°C (350°F) on a kitchen thermometer. Pat dry the whole capers, then add to the oil and fry for 1–2 minutes, until crispy. Remove using a slotted spoon and drain on paper towel. Set aside to cool completely.

Next, working in batches, fry the croquettes for 3–4 minutes, until crispy and golden brown. Drain on paper towel to remove any excess oil.

Scatter the fried capers over the lemony mayonnaise and serve with the croquettes, with lemon wedges for squeezing over.

～～～～

PREP IS YOUR BEST FRIEND:
The croquette mixture can be made the day before and stored in an airtight container in the fridge. You can also crumb the croquettes the day before or call a friend over for an early wine before everyone else arrives and set up a crumbing station. It's a labour of love, but with help it's an easy process.

PERFECTLY PAIRED WITH:
Iceberg and graviera salad with tarragon buttermilk dressing (see page 134).

Crispy calamari with ouzo & oregano yoghurt

500 g (1 lb 2 oz) cleaned whole calamari with tentacles

75 g (½ cup) plain (all-purpose) flour, sifted

1 tablespoon dried oregano, plus extra to serve

2 teaspoons salt flakes

vegetable oil, for deep-frying

OUZO AND OREGANO YOGHURT

200 g (7 oz) Greek-style yoghurt

2 teaspoons ouzo

2 tablespoons oregano leaves, roughly chopped

zest and juice of 1 small lemon

salt flakes and freshly cracked black pepper

Every summer when we visit Greece calamari is on rotation! There is something so delicious about the calamari in Greece, it's freshly caught and somehow manages to complement every other plate on the table.

Slice the calamari into 1 cm (½ in) thick rings.

For the ouzo and oregano yoghurt, combine the ingredients in a small bowl and season with salt flakes and cracked black pepper. Set aside until needed.

In a large bowl, toss the calamari with the flour, oregano and salt flakes until well coated.

Half-fill a saucepan with vegetable oil and heat to 180°C (350°F) on a kitchen thermometer. Working in batches, deep-fry the calamari for 2–3 minutes, until golden and crispy. Remove using a slotted spoon and drain on paper towel.

Scatter the fried calamari with extra dried oregano and serve with the ouzo and oregano yoghurt for dipping.

PREP IS YOUR BEST FRIEND:
The ouzo and oregano yoghurt can be made the day before and stored in an airtight container in the fridge.

PERFECTLY PAIRED WITH:
Our OG Greek saláta (see page 133).

BIG PLATES

MEGÁLA PIÁTA

The Greeks like to eat their largest meal of the day around 3 pm, and enjoy a lighter meal – perhaps grilled fish, horta (greens) and a Greek salad, followed by something sweet like ice cream – later in the evening at about 10 pm (if you turn up to a restaurant in Greece before 9 pm, it will most likely be empty!). If you have been to a Greek dinner party, you will know that most of the food is shared and passed around the table. We love to serve most of our main dishes on large serving plates, as it really removes that stress of dishing up when you have a group of people coming over. The most enjoyable dishes are the ones you can throw in the middle of the table and everyone comes back for seconds, such as moussaka, which all of our friends adore.

Big plates bring people together, whether you're taking a plate to a mate's place or simply sharing a meal with loved ones.

Yiayia's cheesy garlic & butter makaronia

500 g (1 lb 2 oz) packet Melissa #2 pasta
or bucatini

120 g (4½ oz) unsalted butter

80 ml (⅓ cup) extra virgin olive oil

3 teaspoons mashed Jammy garlic
(see page 207)

80 g (2¾ oz) kasseri cheese, grated,
plus extra to serve

large handful of parsley, leaves picked
and finely chopped

freshly cracked black pepper, to serve

~~~~~~

PREP IS YOUR BEST FRIEND:

The pasta can be boiled in the morning
and left to sit at room temperature.
Drizzle with oil to avoid the pasta
sticking together.

PERFECTLY PAIRED WITH:

Yiayia would serve the makaronia with
freshly sliced watermelon and rockmelon
(cantaloupe).

Yiayia Koula would always whip up quick after-school meals for us – Mum
was so grateful for her cooking – and this was the meal we would request
when we felt sick. It's filled with the three greatest ingredients to ever exist:
butter, pasta and cheese.

This is a very speedy recipe – 15 minutes is all you need to get this cheesy,
buttery goodness on the table, although be mindful of the people you invite
over, as the pasta can be very noisy to consume … it definitely brings back
childhood memories for us. Melissa brand pasta is imported from Greece and
these days it is easy to find at most Greek delis. It is our favourite dried pasta
to buy, but feel free to substitute any other spaghetti if you can't get your
hands on any.

Bring a large saucepan of salted water to the boil. Cook the pasta according
to the packet instructions. Drain, reserving 60 ml (¼ cup) of the pasta water.

Meanwhile, heat the butter, oil and garlic in a large saucepan over low heat
and cook for 10 minutes or until the butter and garlic are golden brown.
Add the warm pasta to the pan, along with the reserved pasta water, the
cheese and parsley and give everything a good stir, making sure you coat
every piece of pasta with the delicious garlic butter. Finish with cracked
black pepper and, of course, extra grated cheese.

Place the pot of pasta in the middle of the table and go wild!

Prawn & zucchini risotto

2 tablespoons olive oil

60 g (2 oz) unsalted butter

1 brown onion, finely chopped

2 garlic cloves, crushed

handful of parsley leaves, plus
    1 tablespoon finely chopped
    parsley stalks

1 teaspoon salt flakes

400 g (14 oz) arborio rice

125 ml (½ cup) white wine

6 zucchini (courgette) flowers, stamens
    removed, stems finely chopped and
    leaves torn,

½ bunch chives, finely chopped

PRAWN STOCK

80 ml (⅓ cup) olive oil

1 kg (2 lb 3 oz) large raw prawns (shrimp),
    peeled, tails left intact, heads and
    shells reserved

1 onion, roughly chopped

2 garlic cloves, chopped

1 celery stalk, chopped

1 carrot, roughly chopped

1 bay leaf

1 teaspoon black peppercorns

2 teaspoons tomato paste (concentrated
    puree)

2 litres (2 qts) boiling water

'Al dente' can either be someone's worst nightmare or the perfect way to eat risotto. It can be a scary dish to make – we remember watching *MasterChef* back when it started and the judges calling it the 'death dish'. We promise this recipe is simple to follow and full of flavour. Sit back, relax and have a glass of wine ready to go!

To make the prawn stock, heat the olive oil in a large saucepan over medium–high heat, add the prawn heads and shells and cook, stirring with a wooden spoon to break the shells up in the pan, for about 5 minutes, until roasted and browned. Add the onion, garlic, celery, carrot, bay leaf and peppercorns and cook for a further 5 minutes. Add the tomato paste and cook for 1 minute, then pour in the boiling water. Reduce the heat to low and simmer for 20–25 minutes, skimming off the foam that rises to the surface, until the stock is reduced to about 1.5 litres (51 fl oz). Strain the stock through a fine-mesh sieve and discard the solids, then set the stock aside and keep hot.

Heat half the oil and half the butter in a large heavy-based saucepan over medium–low heat. Add the onion, garlic, parsley stalks and salt flakes and cook for 6–8 minutes, until the onion is soft and caramelised. Add the rice and stir for 2–3 minutes, until well coated in the mixture, then add the wine and cook, stirring, until it is absorbed by the rice. Stir in 250 ml (1 cup) of the prawn stock and continue to cook, stirring constantly and allowing the stock to absorb before adding more, until the rice is al dente and you have a thick risotto – this will take 20–25 minutes. In the last 5 minutes of cooking, roughly chop half the prawns and fold through the risotto, along with the parsley leaves, zucchini stems and remaining butter.

Heat the remaining oil in a large frying pan over medium–high heat, add the remaining prawns and pan-fry for 1–2 minutes, until just cooked through. Serve the risotto immediately, topped with the pan-fried prawns, zucchini flowers and chives.

~~~~

PREP IS YOUR BEST FRIEND:

The prawn stock can be made the day before – cool completely before storing in the fridge.

PERFECTLY PAIRED WITH:

A glass of Alpha Estate Assyrtiko from Florina in the northern part of Greece.

Avgolemono

LEMON CHICKEN SOUP

2 kg (4 lb 6 oz) whole chicken

165 g (1 cup) small star-shaped pasta

2 eggs

60 ml (¼ cup) freshly squeezed
    lemon juice

salt flakes and freshly cracked
    black pepper

extra virgin olive oil, for drizzling

~~~~~~

PREP IS YOUR BEST FRIEND:

The chicken stock can be made the day
before. Allow to cool completely before
storing in the fridge. Store the shredded
chicken in a container in the fridge.

PERFECTLY PAIRED WITH:

Lemon thyme psomí (see page 42).

This soup brings pure comfort and joy to our souls. Avgolemono is a
traditional Greek soup which uses a whole chicken, plus lemon juice and eggs.
As children, whenever we felt sick it was always like the world was ending.
Mum would make us this soup, and after a couple of bowls, everything was fine.

Place the chicken and 3 litres (3 qts) of water in a large saucepan over
high heat and bring to the boil. Reduce the heat to a simmer and cook the
chicken for 1 hour, skimming off any foam that rises to the surface. Using
tongs, carefully remove the chicken from the broth and allow to cool slightly.
Remove the flesh from the chicken and shred into small pieces. Discard the
bones and skin.

Pour the chicken broth through a fine-mesh sieve into a large clean saucepan
and bring to the boil over high heat. Add the pasta and simmer for 6 minutes
or until cooked through. Reduce the heat to low.

Meanwhile, whisk the eggs and lemon juice in a large bowl for about 5 minutes,
until frothy. Slowly whisk in 125 ml (½ cup) of the hot broth (without the
pasta) until combined. Don't do this too quickly or the egg may scramble.

Pour the egg mixture into the chicken broth and gently stir until combined.
Add the shredded chicken, season to taste with salt flakes and warm through.

Divide the avgolemono among bowls, top with a good amount of cracked
black pepper and a drizzle of olive oil, and serve.

Creamy mushroom tarhana

15 g (⅛ oz) dried porcini mushrooms

1 litre (4 cups) boiling water

50 g (1¾ oz) unsalted butter, chopped

60 ml (¼ cup) olive oil

1 brown onion, roughly chopped

3 garlic cloves, crushed

5 sprigs thyme, leaves picked, plus extra
   to serve

2 teaspoons salt flakes

350 g (12½ oz) brown mushrooms,
   finely sliced

345 g (2 cups) dried sour tarhana

375 g (1½ cups) Greek-style yoghurt

100 g (3½ oz) kefalotyri, grated, plus
   extra to serve

freshly cracked black pepper

~~~~~~~

PREP IS YOUR BEST FRIEND:

It's best to make this dish fresh, as it can
dry out if left for too long. If you are short
on time, make it up to the point where
you add the tarhana, then stir through the
yoghurt and cheese just before serving.

PERFECTLY PAIRED WITH:

Lemon horta (see page 153).

Tarhana is one of Greece's superfoods, made with either cracked wheat or
wheat flour and boiled with goat's milk or yoghurt. The mixture is then broken
up and left to dry in the sun, then passed through a coarse sieve and dried for
another two days, by which time the tarhana is completely dehydrated. It is
usually made during summer when the days are hot – the perfect conditions
for drying out the tarhana morsels.

Tarhana can be sweet or sour. Sweet tarhana is made with mostly goat or
sheep's milk and is usually served at breakfast, topped with honey, fruit or jam.
Sour tarhana is made with yoghurt or buttermilk and used in savoury dishes,
as we have done here with mushrooms. We usually fill our suitcases with bags
of the stuff when we go to Greece, but you should find it at good-quality Greek
and European delis.

Soak the porcini mushrooms in the boiling water for 10 minutes, then remove
the mushrooms and finely chop. Reserve the mushroom liquid.

Heat the butter, olive oil, onion, garlic, thyme leaves and salt flakes in a
saucepan over low heat and cook, stirring occasionally, for 10 minutes or until
the onion is soft and fragrant.

Increase the heat to medium, add the reserved porcini mushroom and
cook for 5 minutes or until fragrant and lightly caramelised. Add the brown
mushroom and cook, stirring occasionally, for a further 5 minutes or until soft.
Remove 2 tablespoons of the mushroom and set aside for a garnish. Add the
tarhana and reserved mushroom stock and bring to a simmer, then cover
with a lid and cook, stirring occasionally, for 8 minutes or until the mixture
is creamy and the tarhana is soft. Remove the lid and turn off the heat, then
stir through the yoghurt and cheese.

Divide the tarhana among plates, top with a few extra thyme leaves, some
cracked black pepper, the reserved mushroom and extra grated cheese,
and serve.

Kotopita & pumpkin pie with olive oil pastry

CHICKEN AND PUMPKIN PIE

1 kg (2 lb 3 oz) butternut pumpkin (winter squash), peeled and cut into 2 cm (¾) chunks

80 ml (⅓ cup) extra virgin olive oil

½ teaspoon ground cinnamon

½ teaspoon sweet paprika

2 teaspoons salt flakes

1 brown onion, finely chopped

2 teaspoons mashed Jammy garlic (see page 207)

6 golden Greek pepperoncini, drained and finely chopped

1 teaspoon dried oregano, plus extra for sprinkling

500 g (1 lb 2 oz) chicken thigh fillets, cut into 2 cm (¾ in) chunks

2 teaspoons plain (all-purpose) flour

250 ml (1 cup) chicken stock

200 g (7 oz) goat's cheese, crumbled

60 g (2 oz) kefalotyri, finely grated

OLIVE OIL PASTRY

225 g (1½ cups) plain (all-purpose) flour, sifted, plus extra for dusting

60 g (2 oz) wholemeal (whole-wheat) rye flour

1 teaspoon salt flakes

1 tablespoon white wine vinegar

80 ml (⅓ cup) extra virgin olive oil, plus extra for brushing

Everyone loves a good chicken pie, and we have to admit that this recipe is super delicious and very popular with our friends. The olive oil pastry cooks so beautifully in the oven, and the addition of rye flour gives it a nutty taste with a crisp, flaky finish. Adding warm spices, such as cinnamon, also gives the pie a hint of sweetness that complements the pumpkin.

Preheat the oven to 180°C (350°F). Line a baking tray with baking paper and grease a 26 cm × 3 cm deep (10¼ in × 1¼ in) round baking dish. In a bowl, toss together the pumpkin, half the olive oil, spices and salt flakes. Spread the pumpkin over the prepared tray and roast for 30 minutes or until cooked through and lightly caramelised.

Meanwhile, heat the remaining olive oil in a large saucepan over medium heat, add the onion and saute for 10 minutes or until soft. Add the garlic, pepperoncini and oregano and continue to cook for 2 minutes, then add the chicken and cook, stirring frequently, for 8 minutes or until browned. Stir through the flour for 1 minute, then pour in the chicken stock, reduce the heat to medium–low and simmer for 30 minutes or until the stock has reduced and thickened slightly. Stir through the roasted pumpkin and goat's cheese, then transfer the mixture to the prepared baking dish and set aside to cool.

To make the olive oil pastry, place the flours and salt flakes in a large bowl. Make a well in the centre, add the vinegar, oil and 100 ml (3½ fl oz) of warm water, then use your hands to bring the dough together and knead for 10 minutes until you have a smooth dough ball. Cover with plastic wrap and chill in the fridge for 30 minutes. Lightly dust a work surface with flour, then roll the dough out to a 35 cm (13¾ in) circle about 3 mm (⅛ in) thick.

Scatter the kefalotyri over the cooled filling, then carefully drape the pastry over the top and press the edge to seal. Trim any overhanging pastry and brush the top with a little oil and a sprinkle of extra dried oregano. Use a sharp knife to make a small cross in the centre for steam to escape, then bake the pie for 40–45 minutes, until the pastry is golden and crisp.

~~~~~~

PREP IS YOUR BEST FRIEND: The pastry can be made the day before and stored in the fridge. Allow to come to room temperature for 30 minutes before baking. The filling can also be made a day ahead, but stir through the pumpkin and goat's cheese just before assembling the pie.

PERFECTLY PAIRED WITH: Iceberg & graviera salad with tarragon buttermilk dressing (see page 134).

Yemista

STUFFED VEGETABLES

6 mixed bell peppers (capsicums)

8 large truss tomatoes

2 tablespoons extra virgin olive oil,
plus extra for drizzling

1 brown onion, chopped

3 garlic cloves, crushed

500 g (1 lb 2 oz) minced (ground) lamb

2 tablespoons dried oregano

½ teaspoon ground cinnamon

pinch of freshly grated nutmeg

35 g (¼ cup) pine nuts

½ bunch parsley, leaves picked
and chopped

salt flakes and freshly cracked
black pepper

400 g (2 cups) medium-grain rice

1 litre (4 cups) boiling water

50 g (1¾ oz) Greek feta, crumbled

50 g (1¾ oz) mizithra cheese, finely
grated

dill fronds, to serve

This centuries-old recipe is one of Greece's most famous dishes. Yemista means 'stuffed vegetables', and this recipe can also be made without the mince for a vegetarian option. We love making yemista in summer when tomatoes are at their ripest. You can also use other vegetables such as potato, zucchini (courgette) and onion.

Slice the tops off the peppers and tomatoes and set aside. Using a spoon, remove the seeds and membrane from the peppers and discard. Scrape the inside of the tomatoes onto a chopping board and chop the flesh. Set aside.

Heat the olive oil, onion and garlic in a frying pan over medium heat and cook, stirring occasionally, for 10 minutes or until the onion is soft. Add the mince and cook, breaking it up with a wooden spoon, for 10 minutes or until the meat is browned. Stir through the oregano, cinnamon, nutmeg, pine nuts, tomato flesh and parsley, and season with salt flakes and cracked black pepper.

Preheat the oven to 180°C (350°F). Grease a large baking dish.

Add the rice to the pan, followed by the boiling water, and stir through. Cook the rice, covered with a lid and stirring occasionally, for 20–25 minutes, until tender. Stir through the feta and remove from the heat.

Spoon the lamb and rice mixture into the hollowed-out bell peppers and tomatoes, filling them to the top. Place the tops back on the vegetables, then transfer to the prepared dish. Drizzle the yemista with oil, then bake for 45 minutes or until the vegetables are soft and golden.

Serve the yemista hot with the grated mizithra and a few dill fronds scattered over the top.

PREP IS YOUR BEST FRIEND:
If she had family coming over, Yiayia would sometimes make the yemista the day before. We think they taste even better the next day, as the rice has had more time to absorb all the flavours.

PERFECTLY PAIRED WITH:
Our OG Greek saláta (see page 133) and a glass of Alpha Estate Xinomavro.

Spanakorizo with tomatoes & piperiés

A FEAST FOR
4–6

SPINACH RICE

80 ml (⅓ cup) olive oil

1 brown onion, finely chopped

1 tablespoon mashed Jammy garlic
(see page 207)

2 teaspoons dried oregano

½ teaspoon ground cinnamon

1 tablespoon salt flakes

freshly cracked black pepper

1 bunch English spinach, washed well,
chopped into 5 cm (2 in) pieces

300 g (1½ cups) long-grain rice

625 ml (2½ cups) vegetable stock

zest and juice of 1 large lemon

250 g (9 oz) cherry tomatoes, halved

1 whole Roasted red piperi (see page 211)
or store-bought roasted red bell
pepper (capsicum), finely chopped

½ bunch dill fronds, chopped, plus extra
to serve

~~~~~

PERFECTLY PAIRED WITH:
Fasolakia with tomato and artichokes
(see page 110).

This dish is a vegetarian's dream. Traditionally, this recipe is only made with spinach and rice, hence the name, but we've taken it to another level and jazzed it up with some tomatoes and peppers. If you like, you can also add some crumbled feta to serve.

Heat the olive oil in a large saucepan over medium–low heat, add the onion and jammy garlic and cook, stirring occasionally, for 10 minutes or until the onion is soft and caramelised. Stir through the oregano, cinnamon, salt flakes and some cracked black pepper and cook for a further 2 minutes. Add the spinach and cook, stirring, for 2 minutes or until just wilted, then stir through the rice and stock, cover with a lid and cook for 25 minutes or until the rice is tender.

Remove the pan from the heat and allow the spanakorizo to stand, uncovered, for 5 minutes. Stir through the lemon zest and juice, along with the cherry tomato, piperi and dill until well combined. Scatter extra dill fronds over the top and serve.

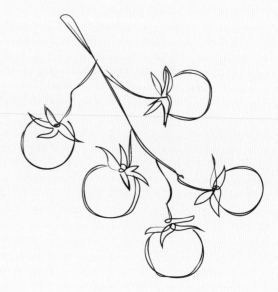

Fasolakia with tomato & artichokes

GREEK GREEN BEANS

80 ml (⅓ cup) extra virgin olive oil

1 large brown onion, roughly chopped

3 garlic cloves, sliced

salt flakes and freshly cracked
    black pepper

60 g (¼ cup) tomato paste (concentrated
    puree)

450 g (1 lb) desiree potatoes, peeled
    and cut into chunks

350 g (12½ oz) frozen artichokes

300 g (10½ oz) long green beans,
    trimmed

400 g (14 oz) tin crushed tomatoes

500 ml (2 cups) boiling water

crusty bread, to serve

Most of our Greek friends agree that their yiayia has cooked them this dish at one time or another. It's a homely favourite that's been made in Greek kitchens for many years. A rich tomato sauce with green beans, potatoes and artichokes is a hug in a bowl. The artichokes we use are Ainos brand, found in Greek specialty supermarkets in the freezer section. They are a little pricey, but you can get two meals from the one packet. If artichokes are in season and you have time to clean and prep them, then go for it!

This recipe is our go-to for vegetarian dinners, it's a dish we love to prepare for friends who want something filling but also full of flavour. Don't forget to soak up all those delicious juices with some crusty bread.

Heat the olive oil in a large saucepan over medium heat, add the onion and garlic and cook, stirring occasionally, for 8–10 minutes, until the onion is soft. Season with salt flakes and cracked black pepper, then add the tomato paste and cook, stirring, for 2 minutes. Add the potato, artichokes, green beans, crushed tomatoes and boiling water and bring to a simmer. Cook for 40 minutes or until the potato is tender and the sauce has reduced and thickened.

Transfer the fasolakia to a serving plate and serve with crusty bread.

PREP IS YOUR BEST FRIEND:
You can make this the day before serving. We also love making it for a simple midweek dinner.

PERFECTLY PAIRED WITH:
Dip slices of Lemon thyme psomí (see page 42) straight into the sauce.

Moussaka, two ways

olive oil spray

1 kg (2 lb 3 oz) eggplant (aubergine), finely
sliced lengthways

650 g (1 lb 7 oz) large potatoes, peeled

2 tablespoons dried breadcrumbs

KASSERI BECHAMEL

80 g (2¾ oz) butter

50 g (⅓ cup) plain (all-purpose) flour

750 ml (3 cups) full-cream (whole) milk

2 egg yolks

80 g (2¾ oz) kasseri cheese, grated

¼ teaspoon freshly grated nutmeg
(optional)

salt flakes and freshly cracked
black pepper

LENTIL BOLONÉZ

80 ml (⅓ cup) Confit garlic oil
(see page 210)

1 brown onion, roughly chopped

3 teaspoons mashed Jammy garlic
(see page 207)

large handful of oregano leaves, chopped

1 teaspoon ground cinnamon

1 teaspoon salt flakes

2 tablespoons tomato paste
(concentrated puree)

2 × 400 g (14 oz) tins lentils, drained
and rinsed

2 × 400 g (14 oz) tins crushed tomatoes

LAMB BOLONÉZ

125 ml (½ cup) Confit garlic oil
(see page 210)

1 brown onion, roughly chopped

3 teaspoons mashed Jammy garlic
(see page 207)

1 teaspoon ground cinnamon

¼ teaspoon freshly grated nutmeg

500 g (1 lb 2 oz) minced (ground) lamb

½ bunch parsley, leaves picked and
finely chopped

2 tablespoons tomato paste
(concentrated puree)

700 g (1 lb 9 oz) tomato passata
(pureed tomatoes)

~~~~~~

PREP IS YOUR BEST FRIEND:
The vegetables and bolonéz can be prepared the day before layered in
the baking dish. You can also make the bechamel a day ahead – simply keep
it in an airtight container in the fridge overnight. The next morning, reheat
the bechamel in a saucepan, stirring over low heat, to loosen slightly.
The moussaka can be cooked 2 hours before guests arrive and reheated
in a 160°C (320°F) oven for 30 minutes or until heated through.

PERFECTLY PAIRED WITH:
The OG Greek saláta (see page 133), of course.

We can eat moussaka for breakfast, lunch and dinner. It's our number-one favourite Greek dish. Our family in Greece always knows to have a tray of moussaka ready for us to eat when we arrive, and by the end of our holiday we have eaten every family member's version. Here is our recipe, which includes a vegetarian and a meat option for the filling. Both are packed with flavour, so don't worry about serving the lentil bolonéz to your meat-loving friends – it's so delicious and hearty. We hope you love them both.

Lightly spray a large chargrill pan with olive oil spray and place over high heat. Working in batches, fry the eggplant slices for 2–3 minutes each side, until chargrilled. Set aside.

Place the potatoes in a large saucepan of cold salted water and bring to the boil. Boil for 15 minutes or until a knife slips through easily. Drain and allow to cool completely, then slice into 5 mm (¼ in) thick slices.

To make the kasseri bechamel, melt the butter in a saucepan over low heat. Add the flour and cook, stirring, for 3 minutes or until the flour has cooked out and the mixture resembles wet sand. Whisking constantly, gradually pour in the milk, a little at a time, until the sauce starts to thicken. Bring to a simmer, then whisk in the egg yolks, cheese and nutmeg (if using), and season with salt and pepper. Cook, stirring constantly, for 10–12 minutes, until you have a thick bechamel.

Meanwhile, to make the lentil bolonéz, heat the garlic oil in a large saucepan over medium–low heat, add the onion, garlic, oregano, cinnamon and salt flakes and cook, stirring occasionally, for 15 minutes or until the onion is soft. Add the tomato paste and cook for a further 2 minutes, then add the lentils and cook for 5 minutes. Add the crushed tomatoes and continue to cook for 8–10 minutes, until you have a thick sauce.

To make the lamb bolonéz, heat the garlic oil in a large saucepan over medium–low heat, add the onion, garlic, cinnamon and nutmeg and cook, stirring occasionally, for 10 minutes or until the onion is soft. Increase the heat to medium, add the lamb and parsley and cook for 5 minutes or until the lamb is browned. Next, add the tomato paste and cook for a further 2 minutes, then add the passata, along with 250 ml (1 cup) of water, and simmer, stirring occasionally, for 30 minutes or until thickened.

Preheat the oven to 180°C (350°F).

To assemble the moussaka, you will need a 24 cm × 28 cm × 7 cm (9½ in × 11 in × 2¾ in) baking dish. Start with a layer of eggplant, then top with a layer of potato, a layer of your chosen bolonéz, then repeat with the remaining eggplant, potato and bolonéz. Spoon over the kasseri bechamel and spread it out in an even layer, then scatter over the breadcrumbs.

Bake, uncovered, in the oven for 30 minutes or until the top is golden brown.

Vine leaf–wrapped flounder with lemon butter

10 large pickled vine leaves

1 × 400–500 g (14 oz–1 lb 2 oz) flounder, gutted and cleaned

1 lemon, sliced

100 g (3½ oz) unsalted butter, chopped

3 sprigs lemon thyme, leaves picked

1 tablespoon extra virgin olive oil

~~~~~

PERFECTLY PAIRED WITH:

Fennel, zucchini flower and mint slaw with currants (see page 140) or Spanakorizo with tomatoes and piperiés (see page 108) as a side.

There is something so delicious about crispy vine leaves. If this is your first time trying them with fish we promise you will love this dish. We absolutely love flounder for its delicate flavour, but feel free to swap it for your favourite fish – flathead works particularly well.

Rinse the vine leaves, then drain and pat dry with paper towel.

Preheat the oven to 200°C (400°F). Grease and line a large baking tray with baking paper.

Line the base of the baking tray with six vine leaves overlapping and top with the flounder. Scatter the lemon slices, butter and thyme leaves over the fish, then fold over the vine leaves and top with the remaining vine leaves to cover. Drizzle with the oil, then transfer to the oven and roast for 20 minutes or until the fish is just cooked through – to check if the fish is cooked, use a fork to carefully peel back the vine leaves; if the flesh is white, it is ready.

Transfer the fish to a serving platter, pour the pan juices over the top and serve.

Mussels with fennel & lemon

2 tablespoons Confit garlic oil
(see page 210)

150 g (5½ oz) unsalted butter, roughly
chopped

1 white onion, finely sliced

1 tablespoon mashed Jammy garlic
(see page 207)

½ bunch dill, fronds picked, plus
2 tablespoons finely chopped
dill stalks

1 fennel bulb, shaved

125 ml (½ cup) white wine

juice of 2 small lemons

1 kg (2 lb 3 oz) black mussels, scrubbed
and debearded

This dish is the sort of food that brings people together. Pop the mussels in the middle of the table and it's a fight to get to the bottom. There is something so delicate and delicious when butter, lemon and fennel come together. We recommend soaking up the buttery juices with fresh crunchy bread.

Heat the oil and 50 g (1¾ oz) of the butter in a large saucepan over medium–low heat. Add the onion, garlic and dill stalks and cook, stirring occasionally, for 10 minutes or until the onion is soft and caramelised. Add the fennel and cook for 8 minutes or until soft, then add the wine and simmer until reduced by half. Add the remaining butter and the lemon juice, and cook for 5 minutes or until you have a creamy butter sauce.

Increase the heat to high and add the mussels to the pan, then cover with a lid and cook, shaking the pan constantly, for 3–5 minutes, until the mussels have opened. Discard any mussels that don't open.

Scatter the mussels with the dill fronds and serve straight from the pan.

PREP IS YOUR BEST FRIEND:
Unfortunately mussels need to be cooked and eaten fresh on the day of cooking.

PERFECTLY PAIRED WITH:
Potato salad with galotyri and green pepper herby oil (see page 136).

Classic slow-cooked lamb shoulder with patates tiganites

1 tablespoon dijon mustard

125 ml (½ cup) olive oil

1 tablespoon Greek spice mix
(see page 206)

1 tablespoon salt flakes

1.8 kg (4 lb) boneless lamb shoulder,
butterflied

2 white onions, cut into 1 cm (½ in) thick
rounds

1 garlic bulb, cut in half horizontally, plus
6 garlic cloves, peeled

250 ml (1 cup) vegetable stock

1 kg (2 lb 3 oz) desiree potatoes, peeled
and cut into wedges

juice of 2 lemons

½ bunch oregano

~~~~~~

PREP IS YOUR BEST FRIEND:

The potatoes can be prepared the day
before and placed in a large bowl of
water. Store overnight in the fridge.

PERFECTLY PAIRED WITH:

Our Roasted garlic and fennel tzatziki
(see page 62). Oregano yoghurt pita
breads (see page 78) are perfect for
mopping up all those delicious lamb
juices, and, of course, our OG Greek
saláta (see page 133).

Lamb is mostly eaten at Greek Easter, but we love lamb all year round!
The best part about this recipe is that you can throw it in the oven and
forget about it, which gives you plenty of time to get yourself ready for
when your guests arrive. Growing up, lamb was always a treat as it was
an expensive meat to buy, so Mum would only buy it on special occasions.
     You need to start this recipe the day before.

In a large bowl, whisk together the mustard, olive oil, Greek spice mix and salt
flakes. Add the lamb and toss to coat completely in the marinade. Cover and set
aside in the fridge overnight.

The next day, preheat the oven to 160°C (320°F).

Line the base of a large roasting tin with the onion rounds and place the lamb
shoulder on top. Using a small knife make six small incisions in the lamb and
insert a garlic clove into each.

Pour the stock into the tin, then cover with a large piece of baking paper,
followed by a large sheet of foil. Transfer to the oven and roast for 2½ hours.

Remove the baking paper and foil and increase the oven temperature to 190°C
(375°F). Continue to cook the lamb for a further 1 hour, basting with the juices
in the tin every 15 minutes.

Scatter the potato wedges around the lamb and add the garlic bulb halves.
Drizzle with the lemon juice and top with the sprigs of oregano, then return
the tin to the oven and continue to roast the lamb and the potato for a final
1 hour or until the potato is tender.

Pork gyros

1 kg (2 lb 3 oz) pork neck, cut into 3–4 cm
   (1¼–1½ in) pieces

4 garlic cloves, crushed

3 teaspoons Greek spice mix
   (see page 206)

80 ml (⅓ cup) extra virgin olive oil

1 sprig rosemary, leaves finely chopped

80 ml (⅓ cup) freshly squeezed
   lemon juice

salt flakes

freshly cracked black pepper

2 tomatoes, halved and sliced

1 red onion, finely sliced

small handful of parsley leaves, finely
   chopped

4 pita breads

200 g (7 oz) Roasted garlic and fennel
   tzatziki (see page 62)

~~~~~~~

PERFECTLY PAIRED WITH:
Fried potato chips and a nice cold
Greek beer.

Even if you've never visited Greece, chances are you have eaten a gyros at least once in your life. This famous dish is Greece's most popular fast food, cooked on a vertical rotisserie and usually made with pork or chicken, and sometimes beef. Served with onion, tomato, fries and tzatziki, and all wrapped up in a pita bread, this is our version of a true classic.

You need to start this recipe the day before.

Place the pork, garlic, Greek spice mix, olive oil, rosemary, lemon juice, 1 teaspoon of salt flakes and cracked black pepper to season in a large non-reactive bowl. Toss well to coat the pork in the marinade, then cover and place in the fridge to marinate overnight.

The next day, place the tomato, onion and parsley in a small bowl and season with salt flakes. Set aside until needed.

Heat a large chargrill pan over high heat and cook the pork for 6 minutes, turning halfway through cooking. Transfer the pork to a plate, cover with foil and allow the meat to rest for 15 minutes.

Carefully wipe the chargrill pan clean using paper towel and return to high heat. Cook the pita breads for 1 minute each side or until charred.

To serve the gyros, spread the pita breads with the roasted garlic and fennel tzatziki, top with the pork and tomato and onion salad, and enjoy.

Mama's lamb manestra

BAKED LAMB CHOPS WITH ORZO

1.5 kg (3 lb 5 oz) lamb chops

80 ml (⅓ cup) Confit garlic oil
(see page 210)

3 garlic cloves, crushed

1 tablespoon Greek spice mix
(see page 206)

salt flakes and freshly cracked
black pepper

1 brown onion, chopped

700 g (1 lb 9 oz) tomato passata
(pureed tomatoes)

875 ml (3½ cups) boiling water

500 g (1 lb 2 oz) orzo (kritharáki)

100 g (3½ oz) Greek feta, crumbled

finely chopped parsley leaves, to serve

~~~~~~~~

PREP IS YOUR BEST FRIEND:
We suggest cooking this just before
your guests arrive so it's nice and hot.
If you have a busy day, you can start
prepping the lamb chops with the oil
and spices and set aside in the fridge
to marinate until you're ready to fry.

PERFECTLY PAIRED WITH:
Roasted garlic and fennel tzatziki
(see page 62) is lovely spooned
over the manestra.

This is the most requested recipe we ask Mum for, even at the age of 33.
She usually has a tray of it ready in the oven for when we arrive home.
The first question we ask her when she picks us up from the airport is,
'What's for dinner?' She always answers, 'Your favourite.'

'Kritharáki' is the Greek word for 'orzo' and it was a staple ingredient
in Yiayia's pantry. Once paired with its best friend 'tomato', it becomes
creamy and saucy. You can opt for pork chops if you prefer pork over lamb;
we love both.

Preheat the oven to 180°C (350°F). Grease a 40 cm × 25 cm × 7 cm
(16 in × 10 in × 2¾ in) baking dish.

Place the lamb chops in a bowl with half the garlic oil and toss with the crushed
garlic and Greek spice mix. Season with salt flakes and cracked black pepper.

Heat the remaining oil in a large frying pan over medium heat, add the onion
and cook for 6–8 minutes, until soft. Spoon the onion into the prepared dish.

Increase the temperature to high and, working in batches if necessary, fry
the lamb chops for 1–2 minutes each side, until browned. Remove the chops
from the frying pan and place in the prepared dish. Cover with the tomato
passata, along with 500 ml (2 cups) of the boiling water, then transfer to the
oven and bake for 30 minutes or until the sauce has thickened and reduced.
Add the orzo around the lamb chops, along with the remaining boiling water,
and cook for a further 15 minutes, stirring every 5 minutes, or until the orzo
is cooked through.

Scatter the feta and parsley leaves over the orzo and serve immediately.

Chargrilled octopus
with Greek salsa verde

1 kg (2 lb 3oz) whole octopus, gutted and cleaned

1 tablespoon salt flakes

1 teaspoon black peppercorns

5 fresh bay leaves

4 garlic cloves

125 ml (½ cup) extra virgin olive oil

juice of 1 lemon, plus lemon wedges to serve

GREEK SALSA VERDE

1 tablespoon baby capers, drained and chopped

1 garlic clove, crushed

100 g (3½ oz) golden Greek pepperoncini, finely chopped

zest of 1 lemon

125 ml (½ cup) extra virgin olive oil

1½ tablespoons red wine vinegar

½ bunch parsley, leaves picked and finely chopped

salt flakes

Halkidiki (where Yiayia was born) is home to some of Greece's most pristine beaches. The northern region is made up of three peninsulas: Kassandra, Sithonia and Mount Athos. At Fourka beach, which is situated on the western-most peninsula, Kassandra, you will find octopus hanging outside of restaurants. It might look odd, but leaving freshly caught octopus out in the sun for at least a day actually helps with the cooking process. But don't worry, this recipe doesn't require you to hang your octopus on your clothesline!

Place the octopus, salt flakes, peppercorns, bay leaves and garlic in a large saucepan and fill to the top with cold water. Place over low heat and simmer for 1 hour or until the octopus is tender.

Drain the octopus and, wearing kitchen gloves, peel away the excess skin. Slice the octopus into large pieces and place in a non-reactive bowl with the olive oil and lemon juice. Set aside in the fridge to marinate for 1 hour.

For the Greek salsa verde, place all the ingredients in a bowl and season with salt flakes.

Heat a large chargrill pan over high heat. Add the octopus and cook for 2–3 minutes, each side, until lightly charred. Cut the octopus into bite-sized pieces, if desired.

Transfer the octopus to a serving platter and serve with the Greek salsa verde and lemon wedges.

~~~~~

PREP IS YOUR BEST FRIEND:

Octopus can be cooked the day before and marinated overnight in the fridge. The Greek salsa verde can also be made the day before, adding the chopped parsley just before serving to avoid the salsa verde discolouring.

PERFECTLY PAIRED WITH:

This dish is perfect for a warm summer's night served with Fennel, zucchini flower and mint slaw with currants (see page 140) and Crispy calamari with ouzo and oregano yoghurt (see page 92).

SA
LA
DS

CHAPTER
04

SALÁTA

For centuries the Greeks have followed a Mediterranean diet
consisting of vegetables, legumes, fish and very little red meat.
This diet is proven to help with longevity and, even better,
red wine is also included!

No matter what season it is, salad is always served on our
table. On the weekend, we head to the local farmers' market
and purchase our weekly shop. We believe it's best to eat what's
in season and support local producers. It's also a lot cheaper.

On a hot summer's night, there is one salad we always crave
and that, of course, is the quintessential Greek salad. Salads
don't have to be boring, and in this chapter we share some
of our favourites that complement all of our big plates.

The OG Greek saláta

200 g (7 oz) cucumber, cut into 1 cm
    (½ in) chunks

300 g (10½ oz) truss tomatoes, cut
    into chunks

1 yellow bullhorn (banana) pepper, finely
    sliced

1 red onion, finely sliced

100 g (3½ oz) pitted kalamata olives

50 g (1¾ oz) caperberries, drained,
    plus 1 tablespoon caperberry leaves

75 g (2½ oz) golden Greek pepperoncini,
    drained (optional)

250 g (9 oz) Greek feta, crumbled

oregano leaves, to serve

OREGANO AND LEMON DRESSING

80 ml (⅓ cup) extra virgin olive oil

juice of 1 lemon

1 teaspoon dried oregano

2 teaspoons mashed Jammy garlic
    (see page 207)

1 teaspoon salt flakes

~~~~~~~

PREP IS YOUR BEST FRIEND:
The dressing can be made the day before
and stored in the fridge.

PERFECTLY PAIRED WITH:
Every dish in this book!

If we had to live off one salad for the rest of our lives, it would be Greek saláta.
No table in Greece is complete without this classic salad and every island has
their own interpretation that often includes a few extra ingredients such as
caperberry leaves or golden pepperoncini. This is our version – don't forget
to mop up all those beautiful juices with some fresh bread.

For the oregano and lemon dressing, place the ingredients in a bowl and
whisk to combine.

Place the cucumber, tomato, pepper, onion, olives, caperberries and golden
pepperoncini in a large bowl, then add the dressing and toss to combine.

Transfer the salad to a large serving plate, top with the feta, caperberry leaves
and a few oregano leaves, and serve.

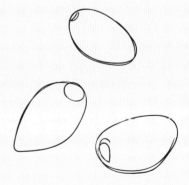

Iceberg & graviera salad with tarragon buttermilk dressing

½ bunch tarragon, leaves picked and
    finely chopped

100 ml (3½ fl oz) buttermilk

1 tablespoon extra virgin olive oil

1 tablespoon freshly squeezed
    lemon juice

salt flakes and freshly cracked
    black pepper

1 iceberg lettuce, cut into wedges

60 g (2 oz) graviera cheese

~~~~~

PREP IS YOUR BEST FRIEND:
The dressing can be made in the
morning and kept in a jar in the fridge.

PERFECTLY PAIRED WITH:
Our Vine leaf–wrapped flounder
with lemon butter (see page 117) or
Chargrilled octopus with Greek salsa
verde (see page 128).

Tarragon can be quite pungent, but we absolutely love it. Once you blitz it
with oil and buttermilk, the flavour becomes quite subtle, making a fresh
and vibrant dressing that works perfectly over crisp iceberg lettuce.

Place the tarragon, buttermilk, olive oil and lemon juice in a food processor or
a blender and process until well combined. Season with salt flakes and cracked
black pepper.

To serve, place the lettuce wedges on a serving platter and drizzle with the
dressing. Finely grate the graviera cheese over the lettuce, season with a little
more pepper and serve.

Potato salad with galotyri & green pepper herby oil

2 shallots, finely sliced

1 tablespoon white wine vinegar

1 kg (2 lb 3 oz) chat (baby) potatoes

180 g (6½ oz) galotyri

GREEN PEPPER HERBY OIL

80 ml (⅓ cup) extra virgin olive oil

100 g (3½ oz) golden Greek
    pepperoncini, drained

50 g (1 cup) parsley leaves and dill fronds,
    chopped

1 tablespoon capers, drained

2 teaspoons white wine vinegar

1 teaspoon salt flakes

~~~~~~

PREP IS YOUR BEST FRIEND:
The potatoes can be boiled the day
before and kept, covered, in the fridge.
The pickled shallot can also be made
a day ahead.

PERFECTLY PAIRED WITH:
Pork and feta keftedes (see page 81) are a
great match for this salad – the meatballs
can be dipped into the galotyri.

This has to be one of our favourite salads – the green pepper herby oil with the galotyri is a delicious combination. We recommend making a double batch of the oil and storing the leftovers in the fridge to add to midweek dinners – it will take them to another level. Pepperoncini can be spicy for some, but you can replace them with mild peppers if you prefer. The galotyri's smooth texture is also perfect with summer peaches drizzled with honey for breakfast. It is sold in most Greek supermarkets, but if you struggle to find it you can replace it with labneh.

Place the shallot and vinegar in a small bowl to pickle for 30 minutes.

For the green pepper herby oil, place the ingredients in a food processor and process until roughly chopped. Set aside.

Place the potatoes in a saucepan of cold salted water over high heat. Bring to the boil, then reduce the heat to a simmer and cook for 12–15 minutes, until the potatoes are tender and a sharp knife slips through easily. Drain the potatoes and set aside to cool completely, then transfer to a large bowl and toss through the green pepper herby oil.

To serve, spread the galotyri onto a serving platter and top with the herby potatoes and pickled shallot.

Beetroot & goat's cheese salad with orange dressing

1 kg (2 lb 3 oz) small beetroot (beets), scrubbed

2 tablespoons extra virgin olive oil

salt flakes

300 g (10½ oz) goat's cheese

50 g (½ cup) walnuts, toasted and roughly chopped

½ bunch dill, fronds picked

ORANGE DRESSING

80 ml (⅓ cup) extra virgin olive oil

zest of 1 large orange, plus 80 ml (⅓ cup) freshly squeezed orange juice

1 tablespoon white wine vinegar

2 teaspoons honey

1 teaspoon salt flakes

freshly cracked black pepper

~~~~~~

PREP IS YOUR BEST FRIEND:
The beetroot can be roasted the day before and stored in an airtight container in the fridge.

PERFECTLY PAIRED WITH:
Kotopita and pumpkin pie with olive oil pastry (see page 104).

We absolutely love this salad combo. The sourness of the goat's cheese paired with earthy beetroots and bright refreshing orange is just divine. We didn't eat beetroot until we were at least 15 years old – we used to think it tasted like dirt – but as we got older we started to appreciate that 'dirt' flavour.

In our first cookbook, *Taking You Home*, we included a delicious roasted beetroot dip that we still make for most of our dinner parties. We really wanted to include it in *Peináo*, but ran out of space. If you'd like to make it, simply place some roasted beetroot in a food processor and blend to a paste. Fold through some Greek-style yoghurt and parsley, season with salt flakes and cracked black pepper, and you have a simple dip that everyone will love.

Preheat the oven to 200°C (400°F).

Place the beetroot on a large sheet of foil, then drizzle with the olive oil and season with salt flakes. Wrap the beetroot tightly in the foil, transfer to the oven and roast for 1 hour or until a knife slips through easily.

For the dressing, place all the ingredients in a bowl and whisk well. Season with cracked black pepper.

Carefully peel the hot beetroot and discard the skins. Cut the beetroot into quarters and place in a bowl with half the dressing. Set aside for 10 minutes to marinate.

Crumble the goat's cheese on the base of a large serving platter and top with the marinated beetroot, walnuts and dill. Drizzle with remaining orange dressing and serve.

Fennel, zucchini flower & mint slaw with currants

6 zucchini (courgette) flowers, stems
finely sliced

2 fennel bulbs, halved and finely sliced
using a mandoline, fronds reserved

2 oranges, peeled and sliced into rounds

½ bunch mint, leaves picked

2 tablespoons currants

DRESSING

80 ml (⅓ cup) extra virgin olive oil

1 tablespoon white wine vinegar

juice of 1 orange

1 teaspoon salt flakes

~~~~~

PREP IS YOUR BEST FRIEND:
The dressing can be made the day before
and stored in a jar in the fridge.

PERFECTLY PAIRED WITH:
Chargrilled octopus with Greek salsa
verde (see page 128).

Yiayia's favourite vegetable is fennel. As kids we remember her slicing it with
a knife and eating it like an apple. We never used to like the aniseed flavour,
but we did love the fresh crunch. This salad is fresh and super tasty, with
a little sweetness from the currants and a slight tartness from the orange.

For the dressing, place the ingredients in a bowl and whisk to combine.

To prep the zucchini flowers, nip the stamens and pistils from the flowers using
your fingers, then gently tear the flowers into strips.

In a large salad bowl, combine the fennel, zucchini stems, orange, mint
leaves and currants. Toss through the orange dressing, top with the zucchini
flowers and fennel fronds, and serve.

Rockmelon, fig & feta salad

2 tablespoons extra virgin olive oil

2 tablespoons oregano leaves, finely chopped

1 tablespoon freshly squeezed lemon juice

1 teaspoon salt flakes

1 small rockmelon (cantaloupe), peeled and cut into thin wedges

4 figs, halved or quartered

150 g (5½ oz) Greek feta, finely sliced

This is the kind of salad we crave in the summertime. Rockmelon is juicy and refreshing, and works perfectly in salads. This sweet and salty match is inspired by the classic watermelon and feta salad, but with our own little spin that uses rockmelon and figs.

In a small bowl, whisk together the olive oil, oregano leaves, lemon juice and salt flakes.

Arrange the rockmelon wedges and figs on a serving platter and top with the feta. Drizzle with the dressing and serve.

PERFECTLY PAIRED WITH:
Serve on a hot summer's day with our Chargrilled octopus with Greek salsa verde (see page 128) and Crispy calamari with ouzo and oregano yoghurt (see page 92).

Roasted eggplant & chickpea salad with minty tahini dressing

1 kg (2 lb 3 oz) eggplant (aubergine),
cut lengthways into spears

125 ml (½ cup) extra virgin olive oil

1 teaspoon ground sumac

1 teaspoon ground coriander

1 teaspoon ground cumin

salt flakes

400 g (14 oz) tin chickpeas (garbanzo
beans), drained and rinsed

½ bunch radishes, trimmed and
quartered

MINTY TAHINI DRESSING

200 g (7 oz) Greek-style yoghurt

2 tablespoons hulled tahini

pinch of ground cinnamon

juice of 1 lemon

½ cup mint leaves, plus extra leaves
to serve

salt flakes

~~~~~

PREP IS YOUR BEST FRIEND:
The minty tahini dressing can be
made the day before and stored in
an airtight container in the fridge.
Stir well before use.

PERFECTLY PAIRED WITH:
Our classic Slow-cooked lamb shoulder
with patates tiganites (see page 120).

We think that eggplant is one of the best vegetables to ever exist! It is super delicious, but it has to be cooked just right – the secret is to use high heat (for perfect crispness) and lots of olive oil (for colour and flavour). To avoid soggy eggplant, we recommend salting the flesh and letting it sit in a colander for 30 minutes – this also helps to remove any bitterness.

If you ever find yourself with leftover grilled eggplant, simply drizzle it with extra virgin olive oil and red wine vinegar, top with chopped roasted red bell peppers (capsicums) and capers, and serve as a delicious mezze.

Preheat the oven to 200°C (400°F). Line two baking trays with baking paper.

Place the eggplant in a bowl and toss with the olive oil and spices, then season with salt flakes. Place the eggplant on the prepared trays and roast for 20 minutes. Scatter the chickpeas over the eggplant and continue to roast for 20–25 minutes, until the eggplant is soft and golden brown and the chickpeas are crispy.

For the minty tahini dressing, place the ingredients in a food processor with 2 tablespoons of water and process until smooth. Season with salt flakes and set aside.

Arrange the roasted eggplant on a serving platter and scatter with the roasted chickpeas, radish and extra mint leaves. Drizzle the dressing over the top and serve.

Endive & manouri salad with preserved lemon dressing

2 teaspoons olive oil

200 g (7 oz) manouri cheese, sliced lengthways

1 small bunch curly endive (frisee), leaves washed

50 g (1¾ oz) sundried tomatoes

PRESERVED LEMON DRESSING

¼ preserved lemon wedge, peel only, finely chopped

2 tablespoons extra virgin olive oil

1 tablespoon red wine vinegar

salt flakes

Manouri is a semi-soft cheese made from the whey of goat and sheep's milk as a by-product of feta. Produced in Northern Greece, where it is often used in Greek pastries or served with a drizzle of honey, its characteristics are lemony and milky. We love pairing it with endive, as it reminds us of Yiayia, who loved this vegetable.

To make the dressing, place the ingredients in a small bowl and whisk to combine. Season with salt flakes and set aside.

Heat the olive oil in a large frying pan over medium heat, add the manouri and fry for 2–3 minutes each side, until light golden and crisp. Carefully remove the manouri from the pan and set aside to cool slightly, then roughly crumble into large chunks.

Place the endive leaves, sundried tomatoes and manouri in a serving bowl, drizzle with the preserved lemon dressing and serve.

PREP IS YOUR BEST FRIEND:
The dressing can be made the day before and kept in a jar in the fridge.

PERFECTLY PAIRED WITH:
Mama's lamb manestra (see page 127).

Grain salad

200 g (1 cup) pearl barley, rinsed and drained

400 g (14 oz) tin brown lentils, drained and rinsed

75 g (½ cup) pumpkin seeds (pepitas) and sunflower seeds, toasted

75 g (½ cup) currants

25 g (¼ cup) flaked almonds, toasted

1 small red onion, finely chopped

½ bunch parsley, leaves picked and finely chopped,

small handful of mint leaves

½ pomegranate, seeds removed

POMEGRANATE DRESSING

80 ml (⅓ cup) extra virgin olive oil

zest and juice of 1 lemon

2 teaspoons pomegranate molasses

salt flakes

~~~~

PREP IS YOUR BEST FRIEND:

The pearl barley can be cooked the day before and stored in an airtight container in the fridge. The dressing can also be made a day ahead and kept in a jar in the fridge.

PERFECTLY PAIRED WITH:

Slow-cooked lamb shoulder with patates tiganites (see page 120).

This wholesome and delicious dish is a staple in our household and our go-to midweek salad. To save time, you can replace the pearl barley with store-bought ready-cooked grains. Don't be afraid to opt for other grains, such as brown rice or farro, and you can replace the brown lentils with chickpeas or tinned beans of your choice.

Place the pearl barley in a saucepan and cover with plenty of water. Bring to the boil, then reduce the heat to a simmer and cook for 30 minutes or until the pearl barley is cooked but still has a little bite. Drain and set aside to cool completely.

To make the pomegranate dressing, whisk the ingredients in a bowl and season with salt flakes. Set aside.

Place the pearl barley, lentils, seeds, currants, almonds and onion in a large salad bowl and toss to combine. Stir through the herbs and dressing, top with the pomegranate seeds and serve.

Lemon horta

BOILED LEAFY GREENS

1 small bunch (about 500 g/1 lb 2 oz)
    curly endive (frisee), leaves washed

juice of 2 lemons, plus 1 lemon extra,
    halved

60 ml (¼ cup) extra virgin olive oil

~~~~~~~

PERFECTLY PAIRED WITH:

Crispy calamari with ouzo and oregano
yoghurt (see page 92) and Orange and
chilli-marinated olives (see page 70).

Yiayia's neighbours used to bring over their homegrown horta and she would
make the most delicious side to go with any big plate. 'Horta' translates to
'weeds' and is used to describe any Greek wild greens, including sorrel,
dandelion, nettles, endive and silverbeet (Swiss chard). The greens are
flavoured with extra virgin olive oil and squeezed with fresh lemon juice.
This simple staple has been served in Greek homes for thousands of years,
and is known to help with longevity.

Bring a large saucepan of salted water to the boil. Add the endive and boil
for 20 minutes, then drain well and transfer to a serving bowl, along with
the lemon juice and olive oil. Toss to combine and serve with the extra
lemon halves.

SWEETS

CHAPTER 05

GLYKA

It is no secret that we both have a sweet tooth, especially when Greek sweets are smothered in honey. When we were young, dessert was always served while we were still eating our lunch or dinner – Yiayia Koula would stand over the sink peeling the skin from a pepóni (rockmelon/cantaloupe) with a paring knife, and offer bite-sized pieces of fruit from the tip of the knife to whoever wanted some. Yiayia would travel to the markets in the morning to collect pepóni, karpoúzi (watermelon) and stafýlia (grapes) ready for when we got home from school. It was the best summer snack to eat while running through the sprinklers or hanging from the clothesline while someone pushed you round.

Ending the night with a sweet treat can leave your guests feeling loved up and very satisfied. If we had the choice between a bowl of spaghetti or a sticky honey pie, we are going straight to the pie. For us, dessert is a must, and no night should ever end without one. Even if your guests exclaim, 'I'm so full', do not listen to them and serve them dessert straight away! Making a couple of different desserts for a dinner party means your guests not only have a choice, but you can divide up the leftovers and send them home with sweet packages to enjoy the next day.

If you're craving something light on a warm summer's night, we recommend our honey and salted almond pagotó (ice cream) on page 157, or for something that will take you to the beach bars of Greece, try our ouzo, watermelon and mint granita on page 187.

Honey & salted almond pagotó

120 g (4½ oz) caster (superfine) sugar

4 egg yolks

250 ml (1 cup) full-cream (whole) milk

500 ml (2 cups) thickened cream

90 g (¼ cup) honey

55 g (⅓ cup) roasted almonds, roughly
  chopped, plus extra to serve

salt flakes

~~~~

PREP IS YOUR BEST FRIEND:
The ice cream can be made the
day before.

We have so many memories that feature ice cream! Summer days in the 90s as kids, the ceiling fan on high, cold face washers delivered by Mum every hour to our bedroom to place on our foreheads, and fritz (a kind of processed meat) and tomato ketchup sandwiches, followed by ice cream, for lunch. Mum would buy us Viennetta, which we called 'fancy ice cream', and Yiayia and Papou would buy the large Neapolitan tubs, with strawberry always the last flavour standing. Our summer days were spent down at Seacliff Beach, as Mum's aunt Jean and uncle Con lived close by. It really is one of Adelaide's most beautiful beaches and it can transport anyone straight to Greece.

If you go to Greece, you will notice small kiosk-like shops called periptero selling ice cream. Choosing one is never easy, but the honey flavour is definitely one of our favourites. This is our interpretation – the addition of almonds and salt flakes takes it to the next level.

Place the sugar and egg yolks in a mixing bowl and whisk for 3–5 minutes, until pale yellow and creamy.

Place the milk, cream and honey in a saucepan over low heat and bring to a simmer. Allow the mixture to gently bubble for 6–8 minutes, until it reaches 75–85°C (167–185°F) on a kitchen thermometer. Add 250 ml (1 cup) of the hot cream mixture to the egg mixture and whisk quickly until combined. Add the remaining cream mixture and whisk until smooth.

Pour the cream mixture back into the saucepan over low heat and stir with a wooden spoon for 8–10 minutes, until the mixture coats the back of the spoon. Transfer to a bowl and set aside in the fridge for 30 minutes to cool.

Stir the almonds and ⅛ teaspoon of salt flakes through the cooled cream mixture, then pour into an ice-cream machine and churn for 1½ hours or until thickened.

Spoon the ice cream into a freezer-safe container and freeze for 2–3 hours. To serve, scatter the ice cream with extra almonds and a light sprinkle of salt flakes. Scoop into bowls and enjoy in the sun.

Yoghurt panna cotta
with sticky grapes

2⅜ titanium-strength gelatine leaves

300 ml (10½ oz) pure cream

2 tablespoons caster (superfine) sugar

1 tablespoon honey, plus extra for drizzling

zest of 1 orange

500 g (2 cups) Greek-style yoghurt

STICKY GRAPES

500 g (1 lb 2 oz) seedless black grapes

2 tablespoons honey

1 tablespoon caster (superfine) sugar

1 teaspoon red wine vinegar

~~~~~~

PREP IS YOUR BEST FRIEND:

The grapes can be cooked the day before, and left at room temperature. The panna cotta can also be made the day before and stored in the fridge, covered with plastic wrap. When ready to serve, remove from the fridge and top with the roasted grapes.

Have you ever thought of roasting grapes? We promise you, once you have roasted your first batch of grapes you will love us for it. Roasting intensifies the flavour by drawing out the liquid, so the grapes taste like sweet jammy raisins. We have used black grapes for this recipe but you can also use red or white varieties. Leftover sticky grapes make the perfect addition to a cheese platter or a salad.

The key to the perfect panna cotta is the right amount of wobble, with a smooth and creamy texture. We use titanium-strength gelatine sheets which we prefer over powder – you'll find them at specialty supermarkets. We have also added yoghurt to the panna cotta to balance the sweetness of the grapes.

You need to start this recipe the day before.

Lightly grease a 1 litre (34 fl oz) serving bowl.

Place the gelatine leaves in a bowl of cold water and leave to soak for 5 minutes or until softened.

Place the cream, sugar, honey and orange zest in a saucepan over medium heat and stir until the mixture is warm. Remove the pan from the heat, squeeze the gelatine leaves to remove the excess water, then add to the warm cream mixture and stir until dissolved. Allow to completely cool, then gently fold through the yoghurt. Pour the mixture into the prepared serving bowl and chill in the fridge for 4–6 hours or overnight, until set.

To make the sticky grapes, preheat the oven to 200°C (400°F). Line a baking tray with baking paper.

Place the grapes on the prepared tray, drizzle with the honey and sprinkle over the sugar and vinegar. Bake for 15 minutes or until the grapes are sticky. Allow to cool completely.

Arrange the sticky grapes, and all the beautiful grape juices from the tray, on top of the panna cotta and serve.

Galaktoboureko with orange syrup

GREEK MILK CUSTARD PIE

1.5 litres (51 fl oz) full-cream (whole) milk

115 g (½ cup) caster (superfine) sugar

1 vanilla bean, split lengthways

180 g (6½ oz) fine semolina

4 eggs, lightly beaten

150 g (5½ oz) unsalted butter, melted

375 g (13 oz) filo pastry

CANDIED ORANGE SYRUP

230 g (1 cup) caster (superfine) sugar

2 tablespoons candied orange in syrup,
    finely chopped

~~~~~~

PREP IS YOUR BEST FRIEND:

The galaktoboureko can be prepared
the day before and kept, covered, in the
fridge. Cook the next day, following the
instructions opposite. The syrup can also
be made the day before and left, covered,
at room temperature. Pour the cooled
syrup over the hot pie.

We have made this Greek milk custard pie countless times for dinner parties, Sunday family lunch, hygge with the girls and nights with Mum. A milk-based custard pie, with buttery layers of filo pastry and dredged in an orange syrup, we call this a big hug on a plate. It's best served at room temperature, preferably on the day it is made. A fun game to play with your guests is to have everyone try and pronounce 'galaktoboureko'.

The candied orange syrup can be replaced with Greek orange marmalade, available from Greek supermarkets.

Place the milk, sugar and vanilla bean in a saucepan over medium heat and bring to a simmer. Remove the vanilla bean and add the semolina in a steady stream while whisking. Continuing to whisk, slowly pour in the beaten egg, then reduce the heat to medium–low and whisk for about 20 minutes, until you have a thick custard that coats the back of a spoon. Remove the pan from the heat and allow to cool slightly, then cover the surface of the custard with plastic wrap (to prevent a skin forming) and set aside.

Preheat the oven to 180°C (350°F).

Brush the base of a 28 cm × 34 cm × 6 cm (11 in × 13½ in × 2½ in) baking dish with a little of the melted butter and top with one sheet of filo pastry. Top with another nine pastry sheets, alternating them lengthways and crossways, and brushing each layer with butter. Pour the custard over the layered pastry and leave to cool for 10 minutes. Repeat the layering and buttering with the remaining six pastry sheets. (Any leftover filo pastry can be wrapped tightly and stored in the fridge for another use).

Using a sharp knife, carefully score the top of the pastry into 12 squares and tuck in any overhanging pastry. Transfer to the oven and bake for 50 minutes or until the pastry is golden and crisp.

Meanwhile, to make the candied orange syrup, place the sugar, candied orange and 250 ml (1 cup) of water in a small saucepan over medium–high heat and bring to the boil. Reduce the heat to medium–low and simmer for 10 minutes or until you have a thick syrup.

Pour the orange syrup over the hot galaktoboureko and allow to stand for 15 minutes. Serve warm or at room temperature.

Apple & raspberry kataifi crumble

80 g (2¾ oz) fresh kataifi (shredded pastry)

110 g (4 oz) unsalted butter, melted

20 g (⅓ cup) shredded coconut

50 g (½ cup) walnuts, roughly chopped

¼ teaspoon mixed spice

125 g (⅔ cup lightly packed) brown sugar

300 g (10½ oz) red apples, peeled, cored and chopped into 3 cm (1¼ in) pieces

1 teaspoon ground cinnamon

250 g (9 oz) fresh or frozen raspberries

vanilla ice cream, to serve

We didn't grow up eating crumble – it just wasn't a dessert that was ever made in our home – but living in share houses as adults, crumble became a dish we made quite a lot. Usually we use whatever fresh fruit we have sitting in the fruit bowl – we absolutely love using plums when they are in season. In this recipe we use apples and raspberries, but feel free to use blackberries as well.

Kataifi pastry is made from a batter that is turned into fine pastry strands. The pastry can be used in sweet and savoury recipes, but traditionally it is used to make ekmek kataifi, a layered dessert with a crispy kataifi base, topped with a thick vanilla custard and finished with a layer of whipped cream and toasted almond flakes. You can find kataifi pastry at Greek and European delis.

Preheat the oven to 180°C (350°F). Lightly grease a 20 cm × 30 cm (8 in × 12 in) baking dish.

Using scissors, cut the kataifi pastry into 1 cm (½ in) pieces, then place in a large bowl, along with 70 ml (2¼ fl oz) of the melted butter, the shredded coconut, walnuts, mixed spice and half the brown sugar. Stir well to completely coat the pastry in the ingredients.

Place the apple, remaining butter, remaining brown sugar and the cinnamon in a saucepan over medium heat and cook, stirring occasionally, for 20 minutes or until the apple has softened.

Tip the apple mixture into the prepared dish and top with the raspberries. Evenly scatter the kataifi mixture over the top, then transfer to the oven and bake for 25–30 minutes, until the topping is golden brown and crisp.

Serve the crumble with ice cream.

Loukoumades with lemon sugar

7 g sachet (2¼ teaspoons) dried
    active yeast

375 ml (1½ cups) lukewarm water

450 g (3 cups) plain (all-purpose) flour,
    sifted

½ teaspoon caster (superfine) sugar

½ teaspoon baking soda

½ teaspoon baking powder

½ teaspoon salt flakes

vegetable oil, for deep-frying

LEMON SUGAR

55 g (¼ cup) caster (superfine) sugar

zest of 2 lemons

HONEY SYRUP

350 g (1 cup) honey

2 cinnamon sticks

~~~~~~

PREP IS YOUR BEST FRIEND:

The honey syrup can be made the day
before and kept at room temperature.
Reheat the syrup for 2–3 minutes before
drizzling over the loukoumades.

This traditional Greek dessert consists of crispy, golden deep-fried puffs
of dough that are soaked in a honey syrup and sprinkled with sugar.
Perfect served fresh and hot, we suggest dragging everyone into the
kitchen after dinner to help out. Have one person on cooking duty, another
drizzling the loukoumades with the honey syrup, someone sprinkling the
sugar over the top and another on washing-up duty.

Combine the yeast and lukewarm water in a jug, whisking to combine. Set aside
for 5 minutes or until frothy.

Place the flour, sugar, baking soda, baking powder and salt flakes in a large
bowl. Pour the yeast mixture into the dry mixture and whisk until smooth.

Transfer the batter to a large greased bowl and cover with a damp tea towel.
Stand for 1 hour or until the batter has doubled in size.

To make the lemon sugar, place the sugar and lemon zest in a bowl. Use your
fingers to rub the lemon zest into the sugar. Set aside.

To make the honey syrup, place the honey, cinnamon sticks and 60 ml (¼ cup)
of water in a small saucepan over medium heat and bring to the boil. Reduce
the heat to medium–low and simmer for 4–5 minutes, until the mixture has
reduced to a syrup. Set aside and keep warm.

Half-fill a large saucepan wtih oil and heat over medium–low heat to 180°C
(350°F) on a kitchen thermometer. Working in batches, drop heaped
tablespoons of the batter into the oil and deep-fry, turning occasionally,
for 2–3 minutes, until golden brown. Remove the loukoumades using a slotted
spoon and drain on paper towel.

Transfer the hot loukoumades to a serving platter and drizzle with the honey
syrup. Sprinkle the lemon sugar over the top and serve.

Portokalopita

ORANGE FILO CAKE

375 g (13 oz) filo pastry

3 eggs

230 g (1 cup) caster (superfine) sugar

150 ml (5 fl oz) extra virgin olive oil

250 g (1 cup) Greek-style yoghurt

1 teaspoon vanilla bean paste

zest of 1 orange

1 teaspoon baking powder

ORANGE SYRUP

250 g (9 oz) caster (superfine) sugar

250 ml (1 cup) freshly squeezed
orange juice

1 cinnamon stick

~~~~~~

PREP IS YOUR BEST FRIEND:

The pastry can be dried the day before
and placed in an airtight container ready
to add to the cake batter the following
day. The cake can be baked in the
morning and left at room temperature.

PERFECTLY PAIRED WITH:

An espresso.

Have you ever stolen a piece of fruit from a neighbour's garden? We have!
There is a bunch of orange trees in Vikki's neighbourhood; it is one of
the first places Greek immigrants moved to when they first landed in Sydney.
Over the years, Vikki has made friends with a couple of yiayias and papous –
their gardens are impressive and full of beautiful juicy fig and citrus trees.
On one sunny Sunday afternoon, Vikki kindly asked a Greek lady for an orange
and she answered no, so Vikki went back an hour later and stole one instead.
It was the juiciest and sweetest orange she had ever eaten, sun-kissed by the
sun and tasting just like Greece.

'Portokalopita' translates to 'orange pie' and is a traditional Greek
cake from the island of Crete. It is made with sweet in-season oranges, filo
pastry and creamy Greek-style yoghurt, soaked in a fragrant orange syrup
to finish. Even though the name of this dish means 'pie', it is in fact a moist
cake. Filo pastry can be intimidating, especially when it needs to be handled
with care, but the great news here is that it's no problem at all if it dries out.

Preheat the oven to 120°C (240°F). Grease and line the base and side
of a 20 cm (8 in) round cake tin with baking paper.

Working with one sheet of filo pastry at a time, scrunch up the pastry and
place in a large deep baking dish, working inwards from one long side.
Transfer to the oven and bake for 30 minutes, scrunching the pastry every
10 minutes. Set aside to cool, then crush the pastry into fine pieces.

Meanwhile, to make the orange syrup, place the ingredients and 250 ml (1 cup)
of water in a small saucepan over high heat and bring to the boil. Reduce the
heat to low and simmer for 15 minutes or until reduced by half and syrupy.
Set aside to cool completely.

Place the eggs and sugar in the bowl of a stand mixer with the paddle attached
and beat on high speed for 3–5 minutes, until light and creamy. Fold through
the olive oil, yoghurt, vanilla bean paste, orange zest and baking powder until
just combined, then stir through the dried filo pieces. Pour the batter into the
prepared tin, then transfer to the oven and bake for 1 hour or until a skewer
inserted into the centre of the cake comes out clean.

Using a skewer or a toothpick, poke tiny holes into the cake and pour the
orange syrup over the hot cake. Leave the cake for 1 hour to absorb the syrup,
then turn out onto a serving plate and enjoy just as it is.

Any leftover cake will keep in an airtight container in the fridge for up to
5 days.

Kourabiedes

CELEBRATION COOKIES

100 g (⅔ cup) blanched almonds

220 g (8 oz) unsalted butter, softened

140 g (5 oz) pure icing (confectioners')
sugar, sifted, plus 125 g (1 cup) extra,
for dusting

1 teaspoon vanilla extract

zest of 1 orange

2 egg yolks

380 g (13½ oz) plain (all-purpose) flour,
sifted

1½ teaspoons baking powder

~~~~~~~~

PREP IS YOUR BEST FRIEND:

The kourabiedes can be made 1-2 days
before your gathering and are perfect for
the days you have unexpected friends
drop by for a coffee.

PERFECTLY PAIRED WITH:

A strong cup of Greek coffee.

We have been baking these cookies with Yiayia since we were six years old,
so they hold a lot of memories for us. Yiayia Koula would bake large batches,
covering her kitchen table with the kourabiedes, ready to be packaged as gifts
for friends and family and even her neighbours. She would place the cookies
on a plastic plate, wrap them in red or clear cellophane and finish them off
with a beautiful ribbon. These cookies are served mainly at Christmas, Easter,
weddings and birthdays, but who said you need to wait for a celebration to
bake them? A crumbly, buttery cookie that melts in your mouth, we guarantee
you will go for seconds immediately after you eat your first one.

Preheat the oven to 180°C. (350°F). Line two baking trays with baking paper.

Place the almonds on one of the prepared trays and roast for 8 minutes or
until lightly golden. Allow to cool completely, then place in the small bowl
of a food processor and pulse until finely chopped.

Place the butter, icing sugar and vanilla extract in the bowl of a stand mixer
with the paddle attached and beat on high speed for 10 minutes or until thick
and creamy. Add the orange zest and egg yolks and beat for a further 2 minutes
or until combined.

Gently fold through the flour, baking powder and almonds until combined.

Roll a heaped tablespoon of the mixture into a 9 cm (3½ in) long rope and
gently curve the rope to create a crescent moon shape. Place on one of the
prepared trays and repeat with the remaining dough to make 26 cookies.
Transfer to the oven and bake for 14–15 minutes, until the cookies are lightly
golden. Allow the kourabiedes to cool completely.

Place the extra icing sugar in a large bowl, add the kourabiedes and gently toss
to coat. The cookies will keep in a large airtight container for 2–3 weeks.

Melomakarona

WALNUT AND HONEY COOKIES

450 g (3 cups) self-raising flour, sifted

180 g (6½ oz) fine semolina

1 tablespoon ground cinnamon

½ teaspoon ground nutmeg

1 egg

115 g (½ cup) caster (superfine) sugar

80 ml (⅓ cup) freshly squeezed
orange juice

125 ml (½ cup) olive oil

125 ml (½ cup) vegetable oil

2 tablespoons brandy (optional)

150 g (1½ cups) walnuts, roasted
and crushed

LEMON HONEY SYRUP

115 g (½ cup) caster (superfine) sugar

175 g (½ cup) honey

2 tablespoons freshly squeezed
lemon juice

DARK CHOCOLATE AND
PISTACHIO COATING

180 g (6½ oz) dark chocolate (70% cocoa
solids), melted

150 g (1 cup) shelled pistachios, toasted
and chopped

WHITE CHOCOLATE AND PINK
PEPPERCORN COATING

100 g (6½ oz) white chocolate, melted

1 teaspoon pink peppercorns, crushed

These delightful rich and syrupy cookies, with flavours of walnut and honey, will definitely satisfy a sweet craving. Melomakarona are usually baked at Christmas or Easter, but we love making them all year round. If you have our first cookbook, *Taking You Home*, you will be very familiar with this recipe.

This time around we have used two coatings for the melomakarona: dark chocolate with pistachios; and white chocolate with pink peppercorns. The pistachios can be replaced with walnuts or almonds, and you can omit the peppercorns and leave them plain, if you prefer. We first tried the white chocolate and pink peppercorn combination in Thessaloniki a couple of years ago; we thought it was a little strange to have peppercorns on a biscuit but, trust us, they're absolutely delicious.

Preheat the oven to 160°C (320°F). Line two baking trays with baking paper.

In a large mixing bowl, combine the flour, semolina, cinnamon and nutmeg.

In a separate mixing bowl, whisk together the egg, sugar, orange juice, olive oil, vegetable oil and brandy (if using). Pour the wet mixture into the dry mixture and stir until a dough forms.

Roll heaped tablespoons of the mixture into oval shapes and place on the prepared trays. Bake the melomakarona for 20–22 minutes, until lightly golden. Transfer to a wire rack and allow to cool slightly.

Meanwhile to make the lemon honey syrup, place the ingredients and 60 ml (¼ cup) of water in a small saucepan over medium heat. Simmer for 3–4 minutes, until syrupy.

Dip the cookies in the syrup for 30 seconds on each side, then return to the wire rack with a baking tray underneath to catch the excess syrup. Sprinkle the melomakarona with the walnuts.

Place the melted dark chocolate in a small bowl and the melted white chocolate in another small bowl. Dip half the biscuits in the dark chocolate and the remaining half in the white chocolate. Sprinkle the pistachios over the dark chocolate melomakarona and the pink peppercorns over the white chocolate melomakarona.

The melomakarona can be stored in an airtight container at room temperature for 3 days, then kept in the fridge for up to 10 days.

Sesame & dark chocolate cookies

255 g (9 oz) brown sugar

120 g (4½ oz) unsalted butter, melted

2 tablespoons hulled tahini

1 egg

225 g (1½ cups) plain (all-purpose) flour, sifted

½ teaspoon baking soda

150 g (5½ oz) dark chocolate (40% cocoa solids), roughly chopped

50 g (⅓ cup) white sesame seeds

~~~~~

PREP IS YOUR BEST FRIEND:
The cookie dough can be made ahead and stored in the freezer for a rainy day. Thaw the dough and follow the cooking instructions opposite.

Cookies served at a dinner party screams fun. Who wouldn't want to eat a warm chocolate cookie after dinner? Tahini is a thick paste made from ground roasted white sesame seeds. People usually associate it with hummus, but it's actually incredible in desserts and the Greeks love to spread it on their morning toast with honey or jam.

The tahini in our cookies adds a rich and nutty flavour that works perfectly with the dark chocolate. If you're having a chilled movie night with a bunch of friends, then these are the perfect dessert to serve. If you really want to take it up a notch, make ice-cream sandwiches with good-quality store-bought vanilla or pistachio ice cream and sandwich a scoop between two cookies.

In a large bowl, whisk the sugar, butter and tahini until creamy and smooth. Whisk in the egg until smooth. Fold in the flour, baking soda and chocolate and stir to form a dough, then rest in the fridge for 30 minutes to firm up.

Place the sesame seeds in a large bowl. Line two large baking trays with baking paper.

Roll 2 tablespoons of the cookie dough into a ball, then roll in the sesame seeds to coat and place on one of the prepared trays. Using your hand, lightly flatten the cookie to a 6 cm (2½ in) circle. Repeat with the remaining dough to make 14 cookies, then place the cookies in the fridge for another 30 minutes.

Meanwhile, preheat the oven to 170°C (340°F).

For soft cookies, bake for 12 minutes or until lightly golden; for slightly crunchy cookies, bake for 14 minutes.

The cookies can be stored in an airtight container for 5–7 days. If you only want to bake half the cookies, store the remaining rolled uncooked cookies in the freezer for up to 3 months.

Milopita

APPLE CAKE

380 g (13½ oz) red apples, peeled, cored
    and finely sliced

375 g (2½ cups) plain (all-purpose) flour,
    sifted

1 tablespoon ground cinnamon

½ teaspoon freshly grated nutmeg

2 teaspoons baking powder

230 g (1 cup firmly packed) brown sugar

4 eggs, lightly beaten

310 ml (1¼ cups) vegetable oil

icing (confectioners') sugar, for dusting

~~~~~~

PREP IS YOUR BEST FRIEND:
Any baked good is best served fresh,
but if you're short of time, the cake can
be baked in the morning and stored in
a warm spot, covered with a clean tea
towel. Alternatively, bake the cake the
night before and reheat in a preheated
150°C (300°F) oven for about 20 minutes.

There are many versions of this cake. Our milopita is light and fluffy and the
perfect morning tea cake to enjoy with a cup of coffee. The name 'milopita'
confuses a lot of people, as the word translates to 'apple pie', but we promise
you it is definitely a cake!

Preheat the oven to 160°C (320°F). Grease and line the base and side of
a 22 cm (8¾ oz) round cake tin with baking paper.

In a large mixing bowl, combine the apple, flour, cinnamon, nutmeg, baking
powder and sugar, stirring to coat the apple in the dry ingredients. Make a well
in the centre, pour in the egg and vegetable oil and fold to combine. Pour the
batter into the prepared tin and bake for 1 hour or until a skewer inserted into
the centre of the cake comes out clean.

Allow the cake to cool slightly, then turn out onto a serving plate, dust with
icing sugar and cut into slices to serve. Any leftover cake will keep, covered,
at room temperature for 2–4 days.

Chocolate & olive oil cake

100 g (3½ oz) Dutch cocoa powder, sifted

½ teaspoon baking soda

125 ml (½ cup) light olive oil

125 ml (½ cup) extra virgin olive oil

125 ml (½ cup) boiling water

230 g (1 cup firmly packed) brown sugar

3 eggs, lightly beaten

150 g (1 cup) plain (all-purpose) flour,
   sifted

OLIVE OIL ICING

50 g (1¾ oz) Dutch cocoa powder, sifted

100 g (3½ oz) pure icing (confectioners')
   sugar, sifted

60 ml (¼ cup) full-cream (whole) milk

60 ml (¼ cup) light olive oil

~~~~~~~~

PREP IS YOUR BEST FRIEND:
The cake and icing can be made
the day before and stored in a large
airtight container.

When Mum would bake our birthday cake it would usually be a recipe straight out of the *Women's Weekly Children's Birthday Cake Book* or something simple yet delicious, like this chocolate cake. Its texture and taste take us back to those classic 90s flavours. This one-bowl cake can be whipped up in less than an hour, with minimal washing up. The olive oil in the cake gives a crumbly moist texture that will have you running back for more.

Preheat the oven to 170°C (340°F). Line the base and side of a 20 cm (8 in) round cake tin with baking paper.

In a large bowl, whisk together the cocoa powder, baking soda, oils and boiling water until combined. The mixture will look like something has gone wrong but once the rest of the ingredients are incorporated, it will become a silky and smooth batter.

Add the sugar and egg to the batter and whisk for 3–5 minutes, until smooth. Stir in the flour and mix until silky and smooth.

Pour the batter into the prepared tin and bake for 55–60 minutes, until a skewer inserted into the centre of the cake comes out clean. Cool the cake in the tin for 10 minutes, then turn out onto a wire rack to cool completely.

To make the olive oil icing, place the ingredients in a small bowl and whisk for 2–3 minutes, until smooth and silky. Pour the icing over the cooled cake, slice into pieces and serve to your favourite people.

Any leftover cake will keep in an airtight container in the fridge for 2–3 days.

Citrus revani

SEMOLINA CAKE

5 eggs

230 g (1 cup) caster (superfine) sugar

180 g (6½ oz) fine semolina

90 g (1 cup) desiccated coconut

150 g (1 cup) self-raising flour, sifted

2 teaspoons baking powder

250 g (9 oz) unsalted butter, melted

1 teaspoon vanilla bean paste

1 tablespoon finely grated blood
    orange zest

2 small blood oranges, finely sliced

CITRUS SYRUP

230 g (1 cup) caster (superfine) sugar

5 cloves

6 strips of lemon zest

2 tablespoons freshly squeezed
    lemon juice

2 tablespoons freshly squeezed orange
    or blood orange juice

This recipe is three generations old – it belongs to our great-grandmother, Vaso. Traditionally, this recipe is not baked with citrus slices on top, but we have added our touch to make it a little more modern. We've used blood oranges but orange and lemon also work nicely.

Preheat the oven to 180°C (350°F). Lightly grease a 20 cm × 30 cm (8 in × 12 in) baking tin and line the base and sides with baking paper.

To make the citrus syrup, place the ingredients and 125 ml (½ cup) of water in a small saucepan over high heat. Bring to the boil, then reduce the heat to medium and simmer, stirring frequently, for 10 minutes or until a syrup forms. Set aside to cool.

Place the eggs and sugar in the bowl of a stand mixer with the whisk attached and whisk on high speed for 5 minutes or until light and fluffy. Add the semolina, desiccated coconut, flour, baking powder, butter, vanilla and blood orange zest and whisk until the ingredients are completely combined.

Pour the mixture into the prepared tin and arrange the blood orange slices on top. Bake for 45–50 minutes, until the cake is golden and a skewer inserted into the centre comes out clean.

Pour the cooled syrup over the hot cake and set aside for 15 minutes before serving. This will allow the syrup to absorb through the cake. You can also serve the cake cool with hot syrup poured over the top – simply reheat the syrup for a few minutes.

PREP IS YOUR BEST FRIEND:
This cake is best made on the day you plan to eat it.

Coffee baklava with dried figs

150 g (1 cup) shelled pistachios, toasted, plus extra to serve

200 g (2 cups) walnuts, toasted

100 g (3½ oz) soft dried figs, finely chopped

1 teaspoon ground cinnamon

80 g (⅓ cup) caster (superfine) sugar

375 g (13 oz) filo pastry

150 g (5½ oz) unsalted butter, melted

GREEK COFFEE HONEY SYRUP

2 tablespoons Oasis Greek coffee

175 g (½ cup) honey

230 g (1 cup) caster (superfine) sugar

~~~~~~

PREP IS YOUR BEST FRIEND:

Baklava is a great dessert to make the day before.

We know what you're thinking, this isn't your traditional baklava, but who doesn't love dried figs? The figs give this baklava a natural sweetness, but if you don't have any, simply replace them with the same amount of extra nuts.

For the Greek coffee honey syrup, combine the ingredients and 150 ml (5 fl oz) of water in a small saucepan over high heat. Bring to a simmer, then reduce the heat to medium and cook, stirring occasionally, for 8–10 minutes, until the sugar dissolves. Set aside to cool.

Preheat the oven to 180°C (350°F). Grease the base and sides of a 20 cm × 30 cm (8 in × 12 in) baking tin and line with baking paper.

Pulse the nuts in a food processor until finely chopped (take care not to overprocess the nuts, otherwise you'll end up with nut paste). Transfer the nuts to a bowl and stir through the fig, cinnamon and sugar.

Carefully lay the filo pastry sheets on a chopping board and trim the sheets to fit the size of the prepared pan or tin. Discard any pastry offcuts. Cover the filo pastry with a clean, slightly damp tea towel, to prevent the sheets from drying out.

Brush one filo pastry sheet with butter, then place in the prepared tin. Repeat with another seven sheets of filo pastry, buttering each layer. Scatter over one-third of the nut mixture and top with another four filo sheets, brushing each layer with butter. Repeat this process twice more. Gently press the final filo layer to compress the baklava slightly. Brush generously with the remaining butter.

Using a small sharp knife, score the top filo layer into 24 squares. Bake for 25–30 minutes, until the pastry is golden and crispy.

Pour the cooled coffee honey syrup over the hot baklava and stand for 1 hour or until the baklava is cool. Using a sharp knife, cut the baklava into pieces along the score marks and serve.

Leftover baklava will keep in an airtight container in the fridge for up to 1 week.

Ouzo, watermelon & mint granita

230 g (1 cup) caster (superfine) sugar

50 ml (1¾ fl oz) freshly squeezed
    lime juice

1 kg (2 lb 3 oz) watermelon, peeled and
    roughly chopped

80 ml (⅓ cup) ouzo

large handful of mint leaves, finely
    chopped, plus extra leaves to serve

The anise flavour of ouzo and the sweetness of watermelon come together in this granita to make the perfect after-dinner digestif that's best served on a warm summer's night. Granita is a frozen dessert that's quite similar to sorbet, except it's made by hand and the only tools you need are a tray and a fork.

Place the sugar and lime juice in a saucepan over low heat, bring to a simmer, stirring, for 5–6 minutes, until the sugar is dissolved. Remove from the heat and allow to cool.

Meanwhile, place the watermelon in a blender and blitz until smooth. Strain the juice through a fine-mesh sieve into a measuring jug (you will need 600 ml/20½ fl oz of juice) and pour into the lime sugar syrup, along with the ouzo and chopped mint, stirring to combine.

Pour the granita mixture into a 1 litre (34 fl oz) capacity shallow tray and freeze for 1 hour. Use a fork to scrape the mixture from the edges of the tray into the centre, then spread out again. Return to the freezer for 30 minutes and repeat the process until the granita is completely frozen into a sandy texture of ice crystals.

To serve, scoop the granita into glasses and top with extra mint leaves.

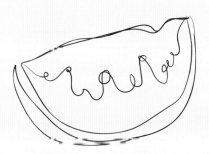

Sour cherry & walnut mosaiko

CHOCOLATE BISCUIT LOG

250 g (9 oz) unsalted butter, melted and cooled slightly

125 g (1 cup) pure icing (confectioners') sugar, sifted

45 g (1½ oz) Dutch cocoa powder, sifted

100 ml (3½ fl oz) full-cream (whole) milk

2 tablespoons brandy (optional)

250 g (9 oz) sweet plain biscuits (cookies), broken into small pieces

60 g (2 oz) sour cherries

80 g (2¾ oz) walnuts, roughly chopped

You'll find this popular Greek dessert in most cake shop window displays. We have given this recipe a little makeover by adding sour cherries and walnuts, along with sweet plain cookies. If you don't have any brandy handy, simply replace it with more milk.

You need to start this recipe the day before.

Place the butter, icing sugar and cocoa powder in a bowl and whisk until smooth.

In a separate bowl, combine the milk and brandy (if using), carefully toss through biscuits and allow to sit for 5 minutes or until the biscuits have absorbed the liquid. Gently fold the softened biscuits into the cocoa mixture, followed by the sour cherries and walnuts.

Place a 45 cm (17¾ in) long piece of plastic wrap on a work surface and top with a sheet of baking paper the same size. Spoon the biscuit mixture evenly along one short edge of the baking paper, then, using the baking paper and plastic wrap as a guide, tightly roll the mixture to form a 26 cm (10¼ in) long log. Twist the ends of the plastic wrap to secure (you may need to double wrap the log with extra plastic wrap to help secure it). Refrigerate for 6 hours or, preferably, overnight to set.

Remove the mosaiko from the plastic wrap and baking paper and use a sharp knife to trim the ends. Cut the mosaiko into 1.5 cm (½ in) thick slices and serve.

Leftover mosaiko will keep in an airtight container in the fridge for up to 1 week.

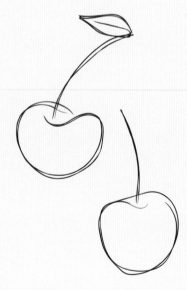

CHEERS

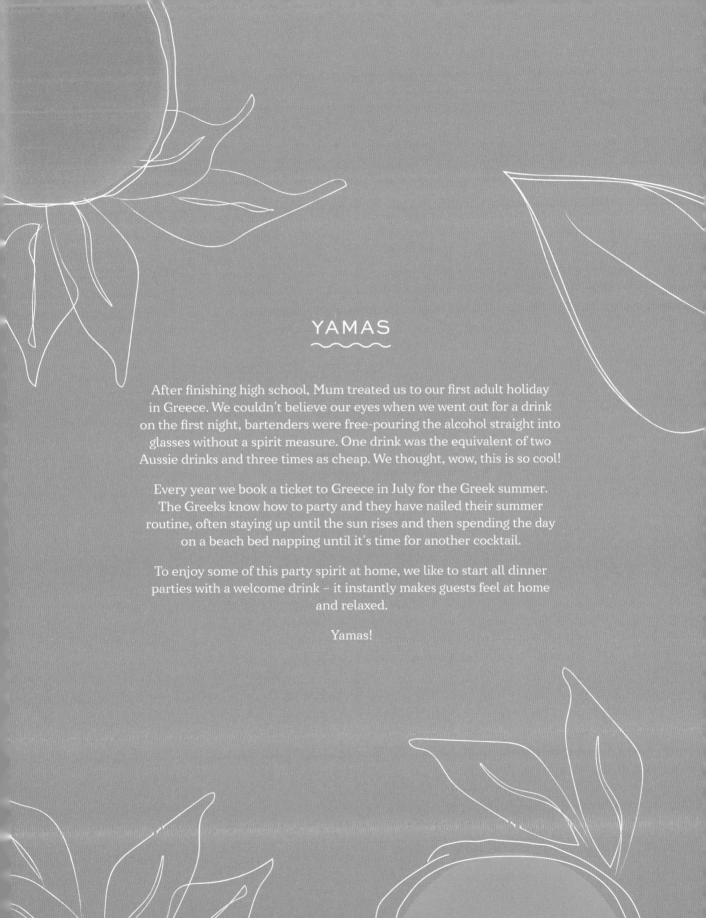

YAMAS

After finishing high school, Mum treated us to our first adult holiday in Greece. We couldn't believe our eyes when we went out for a drink on the first night, bartenders were free-pouring the alcohol straight into glasses without a spirit measure. One drink was the equivalent of two Aussie drinks and three times as cheap. We thought, wow, this is so cool!

Every year we book a ticket to Greece in July for the Greek summer. The Greeks know how to party and they have nailed their summer routine, often staying up until the sun rises and then spending the day on a beach bed napping until it's time for another cocktail.

To enjoy some of this party spirit at home, we like to start all dinner parties with a welcome drink – it instantly makes guests feel at home and relaxed.

Yamas!

Freddo cappuccino

double shot of espresso coffee

2 teaspoons sugar, or to taste

ice cubes

80 ml (⅓ cup) skim milk

Coffee is a big part of Greek culture, and locals are known to spend hours sipping away on the same drink. Our Greek cousins are baffled at how fast we drink our coffee, but just like any coffee order, it's a personal preference of how you like it. The difference between a frappe and a freddo cappuccino is that a frappe is made with instant coffee and blended with water and ice. A freddo uses espresso coffee and is topped with frothy skim milk; some places in Greece even use evaporated milk.

Place a metal milkshake cup in the freezer for 20 minutes.

Place the coffee, sugar and one ice cube into the cooled cup and process in a milkshake maker on high speed for 1 minute or until frothy. Pour the coffee into a tall glass filled with 3–4 ice cubes.

Wash the milkshake cup and add the milk, then process on high speed for 2 minutes or until frothy. Pour the frothy milk over the coffee, stir and sip away!

Mountain tea & lemon iced tea

2 litres (2 qts) hot water

30 g (3 cups firmly packed) dried
  mountain tea leaves

115 g (⅓ cup) honey

170 ml (⅔ cup) freshly squeezed lemon
  juice, plus 1 lemon, finely sliced

ice cubes

½ bunch mint, leaves picked

Mountain tea is a healthy, naturally caffeine-free herbal tea made from a single variety of the *Sideritis* plant. Perhaps unsurprisingly, it is mainly grown in the mountainous regions of Greece, where the local communities are the largest consumers of this beneficial drink. For centuries, Greek shepherds residing in the mountains drank the tea to keep warm and ward off sickness.

We love serving this iced tea during the week if we are hosting a dinner and not drinking alcohol. If someone wants alcohol, it tastes yummy with a shot of gin or vodka. Any leftover tea can be poured into ice cube trays and added to soda water for an afternoon drink.

Combine the hot water and mountain tea leaves in a saucepan and bring to the boil. Turn off the heat and add the honey, and allow the tea to infuse for 15 minutes.

Strain the tea through a fine-mesh sieve into a jug and discard the solids. Stir through the lemon juice and set aside in the fridge to cool completely before serving.

To serve, pour the tea into a 2.5 litre (2½ qt) serving jug half-filled with ice and top with the lemon slices and mint leaves.

Mastiha & basil spritz

2 teaspoons honey

2 teaspoons boiling water

100 ml (3½ fl oz) Skinos Mastiha Spirit

2 tablespoons freshly squeezed
   lemon juice

handful of basil leaves, plus extra to serve

ice cubes

soda water (club soda), to top

With a sweet and aromatic woodiness and refreshing taste, mastiha is the resin released from the skinos tree in Chios, also known as the 'mastic island'. Famous for its healing properties, mastic is one of the most ancient superfoods. A couple of years ago at our favourite beach bar in Fourka, the bartender served us this cocktail. Straight after finishing it we asked him if we could put the recipe in our next cookbook.

Our favourite mastiha to drink is Skinos Mastiha Spirit, which you can purchase online.

In a small bowl, combine the honey and boiling water. Stir to dissolve and cool.

Add the mastiha, lemon juice, basil leaves, honey mixture and a small handful of ice cubes to a cocktail shaker and shake until well combined.

Strain into two tall glasses filled with ice cubes, top with a splash of soda water and garnish with extra basil leaves.

Mediterranean sour

1 tablespoon honey

1 tablespoon boiling water

80 ml (⅓ cup) pure tsipouro

60 ml (¼ cup) freshly squeezed
    lemon juice

1 egg white

ice cubes

2 dehydrated lemon slices (see page 15)

This recipe is inspired by a cocktail from one of our favourite bars in
Athens called Line Athens, which focuses on using local Greek produce
with a no-waste approach.

Tsipouro is a grape-distilled spirit made using leftover grapes from the
wine-pressing process, and is usually served as a welcome drink to guests.
It has a very strong scent but try not to be put off by it, as this cocktail is so
delicious. There are two types of tsipouro: pure and anise-flavoured – we have
used the pure version in this cocktail. You'll find both varieties sold at most
bottle shops and online.

In a small bowl, combine the honey and boiling water. Stir to dissolve and
leave to cool completely.

Add the tsipouro, lemon juice, egg white, honey mixture and a handful of
ice cubes to a cocktail shaker and shake vigorously for 15–20 seconds, until
frosted on the outside. Strain into two sour goblet glasses.

Garnish with the dehydrated lemon slices and serve.

Greek negroni

60 ml (¼ cup) vermouth (we use Otto's
    Athens vermouth)

60 ml (¼ cup) gin (we use Votanikon
    Greek gin)

60 ml (¼ cup) Campari

ice cubes

2 dehydrated figs, to serve

2 dehydrated orange slices (see page 15),
    to serve

We can never go past a classic, and this is our go-to cocktail. We love starting
the night with a negroni. We use Otto's Athens vermouth, which is very
popular among bartenders throughout Greece.

Add the vermouth, gin and Campari to a cocktail shaker and stir with ice until
the liquid is cold.

Strain into two short glasses and top with a large piece of ice. Garnish with
a dehydrated fig and orange slice and serve.

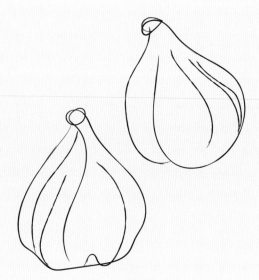

BA
SIC
S

CHAPTER
07

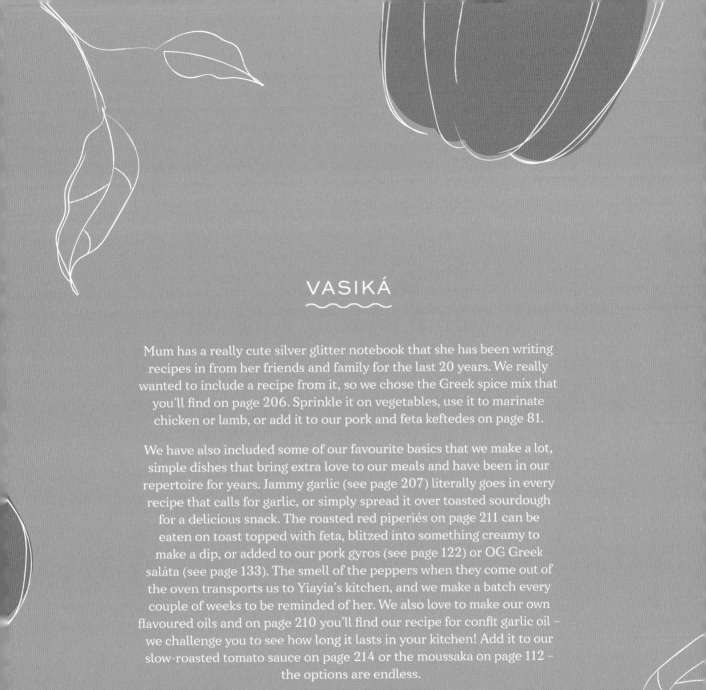

VASIKÁ

Mum has a really cute silver glitter notebook that she has been writing recipes in from her friends and family for the last 20 years. We really wanted to include a recipe from it, so we chose the Greek spice mix that you'll find on page 206. Sprinkle it on vegetables, use it to marinate chicken or lamb, or add it to our pork and feta keftedes on page 81.

We have also included some of our favourite basics that we make a lot, simple dishes that bring extra love to our meals and have been in our repertoire for years. Jammy garlic (see page 207) literally goes in every recipe that calls for garlic, or simply spread it over toasted sourdough for a delicious snack. The roasted red piperiés on page 211 can be eaten on toast topped with feta, blitzed into something creamy to make a dip, or added to our pork gyros (see page 122) or OG Greek saláta (see page 133). The smell of the peppers when they come out of the oven transports us to Yiayia's kitchen, and we make a batch every couple of weeks to be reminded of her. We also love to make our own flavoured oils and on page 210 you'll find our recipe for confit garlic oil – we challenge you to see how long it lasts in your kitchen! Add it to our slow-roasted tomato sauce on page 214 or the moussaka on page 112 – the options are endless.

Greek spice mix

2 tablespoons dried oregano

1 tablespoon dried dill

1 tablespoon dried thyme leaves

1 tablespoon dried basil

1 tablespoon dried mint

1 tablespoon garlic powder

1 teaspoon ground cinnamon

1 teaspoon sweet paprika

2 teaspoons salt flakes

1 teaspoon freshly cracked black pepper

Mum loves making us chicken schnitzels when we are back home in Adelaide; well we kind of tell her that's what we want, but she also knows it's our favourite. This Greek spice mix is great to add to a schnitzel crumb – simply combine a cup of dried breadcrumbs and 2 tablespoons of the spice mix to crumb four chicken schnitzels.

Combine the ingredients in a jar and give it a good shake. Seal with a lid, add a label and store in your spice draw for up to 1 year.

Jammy garlic

3 whole garlic bulbs

185 ml (¾ cup) extra virgin olive oil,
plus 1½ tablespoons extra

Sweet, jammy garlic is a kitchen staple that should stick around forever. We promise you this recipe will be used so often in your kitchen that it will become a favourite in your household. It's so simple to make and the jar sits nicely on your kitchen bench for those days when you want to add a quick flavour bomb to dishes.

Depending on how much garlic you like to use, the amount here should last 1–2 weeks. We love to make a double batch during the week, so we have a jar ready to go on the weekend.

Preheat the oven to 180°C (350°F).

Using a sharp knife, slice the very top off the garlic bulbs, to expose the cloves. Place the garlic bulbs on a large piece of foil and drizzle with the 1½ tablespoons of olive oil. Wrap the garlic tightly in the foil and bake for 45 minutes or until the garlic is jammy and the kitchen smells heavenly.

Squeeze the garlic bulbs to release their jammy goodness, then use a fork to mash the garlic into a paste. Set aside to cool, then transfer the mashed garlic to a small jar and cover with the 185 ml (¾ cup) of oil. Seal with a lid and store on your kitchen bench for up to 1 month.

Greek spice mix

Confit garlic oil

3 whole garlic bulbs

4 fresh bay leaves

375 ml (1½ cups) extra virgin olive oil

Don't worry we haven't used a fancy word here, 'confit' simply means any type of food that is cooked slowly over low heat for a long period of time. Once the garlic has cooled, it becomes like butter and can be spread over sourdough and added to most of our recipes that call for garlic.

The longer you leave the garlic in the oil, the stronger the flavour will be. Garlic oil jars make the best presents for your guests or even for Christmas. Place a tag around the jar with the recipe name and your loved ones will be impressed. Always try to use Australian garlic for best results.

Peel the garlic cloves and place in a saucepan with the bay leaves and oil. Place over high heat until it reaches 60°C (140°F) on a kitchen thermometer, then reduce the heat to low and cook gently for 30 minutes or until the garlic is soft and lightly coloured.

Allow the oil to completely cool in the pan, then gently pour into a 600 ml (20½ fl oz) sterilised jar and seal with a lid. Store on your kitchen bench or in the pantry for up to 3 months.

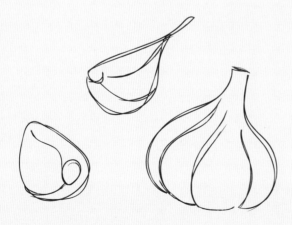

Roasted red piperiés

6 red bell peppers (capsicums)

2 tablespoons extra virgin olive oil,
plus extra to cover

A jar of roasted piperiés is something that we always have in the fridge, they are so versatile and can be added to lots of recipes, or eaten alone as a mezze drizzled with some extra virgin olive oil, red wine vinegar and a few chopped capers. We usually like to make them on a Sunday afternoon, and the smell of roasted piperiés is a smell that transports us straight to Greece.

One of our favourite recipes from our first cookbook, *Taking You Home*, is our Htipiti dip, a simple creamy feta and roasted pepper dip. Simply blitz the roasted piperiés with a block of feta and a couple of splashes of Greek extra virgin olive oil and process until creamy. Serve with pita bread and enjoy as a mezze.

Preheat the oven to 200°C (400°F). Line a large baking tray with baking paper.

Place the bell peppers on the prepared tray and drizzle with the oil. Roast the peppers for 50–55 minutes, until the skins have blistered and blackened.

Carefully transfer the peppers to a large glass bowl and cover tightly with plastic wrap. Set aside for 20 minutes, to allow the steam from the peppers to help loosen the skin. Remove the peppers from the bowl, then peel and discard the skins, membrane and seeds.

Place the roasted peppers in a large jar, making sure they are completely submerged in oil. Store in the fridge for up to 3 months.

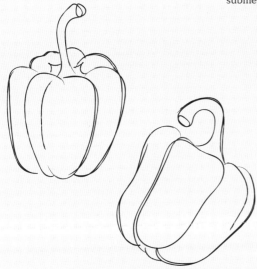

Confit garlic oil

Roasted red piperiés

Slow-cooked tomatoes

500 g (1 lb 2 oz) mixed cherry tomatoes
3 garlic cloves, peeled
250 ml (1 cup) extra virgin olive oil

This recipe starts off as a pan of beautifully cooked tomatoes. Cooking the tomatoes in plenty of oil releases all their sweet juices, and here we've used the same cooking method as the confit garlic oil on page 210. The best part about this recipe is that you get two dishes from it. The cooked tomatoes are perfect for stirring through rice, such as our spanakorizo recipe on page 108, adding to a bolognese or even using as the base for a pizza. The other option is to blitz the tomatoes using a stick blender to form a rich creamy sauce that's perfect for folding through pasta or using in our fasolakia on page 110.

Place the ingredients in a saucepan over high heat and cook until the oil reaches 60°C (140°F) on a kitchen thermometer. Reduce the heat to low and cook for 45 minutes or until the tomatoes and garlic have softened.

Allow the tomatoes to cool completely, then transfer to a large sterilised jar with a lid. Store in the fridge for up to 1 month, making sure the tomatoes are completely covered in the oil.

To turn the tomato mixture into a creamy sauce, place the cooled tomatoes, garlic and oil in a blender, or use a stick blender, and blend to a smooth sauce. Store in a jar in the fridge for up to 1 week.

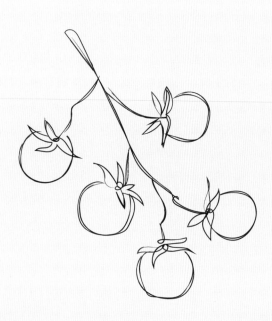

THANK YOU

This book is dedicated to our beautiful mum, Sophie. Without you we wouldn't be where we are today – thank you for always reminding us that 'we got this', for being our biggest fan and raising us to become strong women, just like you. We love you.

To Baba, our father. Thank you for always watching over us and making all of our dreams come true.

To Yiayia Koula and Papou Vasilis, thank you for everything you did for us and Mum, you were there in the moments we needed someone to make us feel like everything was going to be okay. Yiayia, you taught us how to fold a sentóni (bed sheet), iron (basically everything from tea towels and knickers to pyjamas and shirts … you name it), make pastitsio, crumb chicken and, most importantly, how to love and treat everyone like they are family. Papou, thank you for teaching us how to paint, use our manners and to keep our posture in place.

To the man of the family, Luke, who has been a brother figure to Helena and the best husband to Vikki. Thank you for putting up with us, for believing in us and always listening and giving the best advice. You have the biggest heart and without you there would be some life lessons we would have never learnt.

To our family in Greece, Thea Christine, without you Yiayia would not be living the happy comfortable life she now has in Greece. Thank you for being the positive, happy person you are and for always inspiring us to be creative. To Nicole and Alex, thank you for your support and love. We love you so much.

To our hygge girls – Sophia, Rachael and Chloe – thank you for always believing in us and forever supporting us.

We would like to thank those who have helped us create *Peináo*: Paul McNally, Lucy Heaver and everyone else at Smith Street Books, thank you for believing in us and our book; Vanessa Masci, for your delightful design and illustrations; and Jorge, for capturing our food so beautifully – your work is incredible and we love every photo you shot for *Peináo* – thank you for putting up with us for ten days, you became the brother we always wanted.

 helenaandvikki

Helena would like to thank …

To Luke and Terrance, thank you for allowing us to invade your space, and for your ongoing support.

To Phoebe, thank you for believing in me and giving me the opportunity to work at *delicious.* magazine. You taught me what I know today about recipe writing; and to Kirsten, thank you for always inspiring me to think outside the box, and for showing me the way.

To Michelle, thank you for allowing me to turn our house upside down to shoot *Peináo*. You're the best housemate and friend anyone could ever ask for.

And, lastly, to the gods of red wine for saving me most nights, thank you.

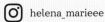 helena_marieee

Vikki would like to thank …

Luke, my husband, thank you for always supporting me, believing in and pushing me to chase my dreams. You have taught me so much and I am the person I am today because of you. I love you so much.

To my in-laws, Leigh and Phillip, thank you for supporting me and always guiding me in the right direction. I am always grateful for your advice and your honest feedback on my recipes.

[Instagram icon] vikki_leigh

INDEX

INDEX

INDEX

Published in 2023 by Smith Street Books
Naarm (Melbourne) | Australia
smithstreetbooks.com

ISBN: 978-1-9227-5459-2

Smith Street Books respectfully acknowledges the Wurundjeri People of the Kulin
Nation, who are the Traditional Owners of the land on which we work, and we pay
our respects to their Elders past and present.

Publisher: Paul McNally
Senior editor: Lucy Heaver, Tusk Studio
Design and illustrations: Vanessa Masci
Food and incidentals photographer: Jorge Rivera
Location photographers: Helena Moursellas and Pawel Soltysinski
Food stylist: Helena Moursellas
Prop stylist: Vikki Moursellas
Food preparation: Helena Moursellas and Vikki Moursellas
Proofreader: Pamela Dunne
Indexer: Helena Holmgren

Printed & bound in China by C&C Offset Printing Co., Ltd.

Book 286
10 9 8 7 6 5 4 3 2 1